Also By Chris Bent

Available in Paperback and Electronic Versions

1-800-I-AM-UNHAPPY
Volume 1

1-800-I-AM-UNHAPPY
Volume 2

1-800-FOR-WOMEN-ONLY

1-800-LAUGHING-OUT-LOUD

1-800-OH-MY-GOODNESS

1-800-FOR-SEALS-ONLY

1-800-OH-MY-DONALD

1-800-FOR-VETERANS-ONLY

1-800-ONLY-FOR-LOVE

1-800-OH-MY-BLACKNESS

1-800-OLD-PEOPLE-MATTER

1-800-CALL-TO-ARMS

controversial writs by

CHRIS BENT

www.chrisbent.com

Published in the USA by Chris Bent
Naples, Florida USA
http://ChrisBent.com

1-800-I-AM-UNHAPPY,
1-800-FOR-WOMEN-ONLY,
1-800-LAUGHING-OUT-LOUD,
1-800-OH-MY-GOODNESS,
1-800-FOR-SEALS-ONLY,
1-800-OH-MY-DONALD,
1-800-FOR-VETERANS-ONLY,
1-800-ONLY-FOR-LOVE,
1-800-OH-MY-BLACKNESS,
1-800-OLD-PEOPLE-MATTER, and
1-800-CALL-TO-ARMS

are trademarks owned by Chris Bent and are used with his permission.

DEDICATION

To Christina, Candice, Courtney, and all of us
who can make a difference when we dare.
As somewhere some guys say, "Whoever Dares Wins."

Prologue

This book is a call to arms. None of us can sit idly by any longer while our nation erodes before our eyes. The chapters are aids to loosening our blinders. What is worth saving must be addressed. Morality is at the heart of the solution. Good is letting Evil play. This is not acceptable.

Chris Bent

Kennebunkport
August 2017
www.ChrisBent.com

Contents

Call to Arms

Who makes the call?

Do we wait for the newspapers? No, they never quite get it. Too involved with sensational spins on minor events.

Sometimes the truth is right there in front of us and we're oblivious to it. We just don't see it.

Inaction is so easy. Until it is too late… This has always been the case.

We think war can be avoided as long as the media has enough non-violent options, however obscure. Endless "what if's" for the front pages.

The handwriting on the wall is mocked… All we see today is graffiti….

We no longer take Evil seriously.

We no longer teach "good" in the schools.

We are seen as confused, hypocritical, and weak by the forces of Evil, the "Armed Forces Of Evil". We are at war

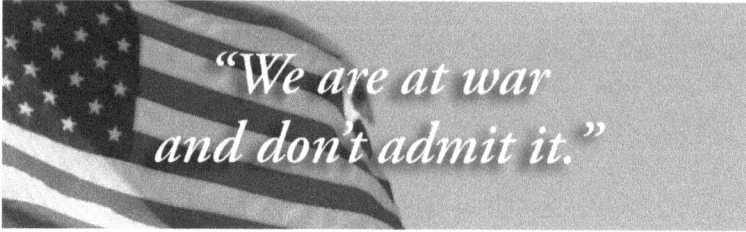
"We are at war and don't admit it."

and don't admit it. Be it on the battlefield with bullets or with hearts.

We have too many distractions… and things to do… and pundits to clarify all that is true.

Violence is still "incidental" and not taken as ominous signals of our jeopardy and our weakness.

Tattoos do not scare away Evil. Nor do labels.

Bureaucracies dither and shuffle paper.

We send our few precious volunteer soldiers into disgusting situations with the expectation that they alone will solve the foreign social dilemmas.

NO..!!! It is not working. And we are not united.

War must be declared before our grandchildren will have nothing but a laptop in a cultural jail.

WAR. WAR. Can we not say the word?

Passing a law or giving 500 million dollars to the United Nations will not do anything at all.

Raise your right arm and solemnly swear you will fight every EVIL right now.

You see it… admit it…. Stop doing nothing.

This is your Call To Arms.

Man up.

Walls R Us

"Hey guys, what is all the self-righteous indignation about having borders that work?

Why don't you spend one week in Aleppo, Syria and tell me we don't have a problem.

Build the damn wall and then say it was a big mistake. Why everyone and the media is so negative beats me... Go positive and do something.

But it is more about who we are, and how we become who we want to be. I don't feel secure these days. Travel outside the USA is of a concern. Look at what is happening in Europe. Much less the Middle-East.... Our war should not be amongst one another. Let's disagree but be friends.

In combat you become close and learn to pray. We have erected our own wall within. That is the wall to tear down.

Yes, to protect ourselves from what the future looks like.... borders must work. There has to be control.

You want to get in a movie theatre? Then you have to buy a ticket, find a seat, and not be disruptive or you will be kicked out.

Want to get on my airplane flight? I sure hope all are screened.

Walls in homes and buildings screen too.

Walls R Us.

Sanctuary City

It ain't no sanctuary if everyone does not have a home to live in.

It is not government's business to bureaucratize compassion. It is the peoples' business to help people.

There has to be a non-profit like Habitat that finds living sanctuaries. No employment and you have more hidden homeless.

The politics of sanctuary cities is nonsense. Sanctuary is only real if segregation is not the result. Immigration policy must be followed to the letter so that we all know what to expect. Those who have made it here will know their situation is always tenuous until citizenship is achieved. Citizenship and the ability to speak English and say the Pledge of Allegiance from memory should be integral to any affirmation. Our arms must be open with compassion and intelligence. Jobs have to be earned. Vagrancy brings the shadow of deportation. Traditional Latin American family values are solid. Our culture is having a difficult time.

> ## *"Sanctuary is only real if segregation is not the result."*

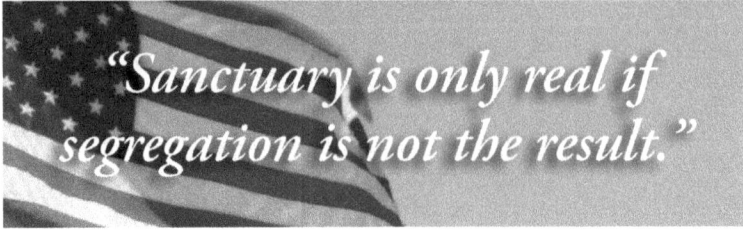

Sanctuary must be in the heart. You feel sanctuary when you are welcomed and embraced. Filling out forms is not the answer. We can only handle the amount we can love.

Why is Extreme Vetting such a big deal??

So what you have to be honest and transparent; then you have less to fear.

Extreme Sanctuary is when you actually take someone into your home.

Hello?

Is that too extreme?

Sensitive Vetting

Feelings come first.

How you feel about the applicant.... Will guide actions.

Immigration staffs must screen for all kinds of behavior... For eye contact... For body language.

And... treat each person as a person.

Manuals and regulations that defy comprehension box the process in...

Terrorism is expanding. Hello?

Do we have to be more diligent than ever?

Would you like to be the immigration agent that lets an eventual terrorist pass through?

To bomb a restaurant? A subway? A movie theatre?

Do we not have to be careful to some extreme?

Our nation and Christianity are under attack.

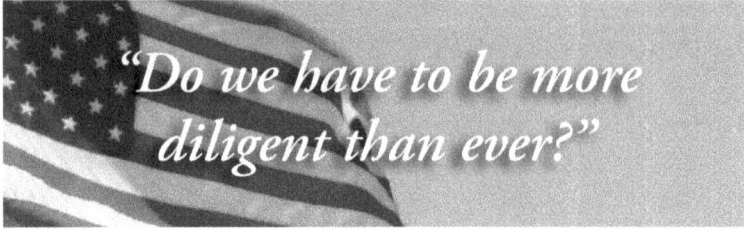

"Do we have to be more diligent than ever?"

Our founding principles are being used against us. Go figure.

Some are outraged and parsing words like the good old days. Whether you call it "extreme" or "intensely strict" or "by the book", does not matter.

Fools get distracted by their own extreme interpretations.

While they dither... we are diminished.

Shut the borders until all agree...

Now isn't that extreme?

Protest Ready or Not

"Olly Olly Oxen Free!" Protest, ready or not, here we come!

Ever play this game as a kid?

We said "Olly Olly In Free!" when we made it back without getting caught... ready or not!

Who ever heard about protests before the media's celebration of them on the news?

If you have a cause, the other person automatically becomes the villain. Once labeled as a villain it is hard to be the good guy again.

Is "Protests 'R Us" the new norm? Violence without options?

Burn a car and you get the front pages.

What is confusing is that there are so many truly serious causes out there that never get recognized. We like to blame the USA for all our problems and immaturities.

"Let's list all the women's abuses that are international..."

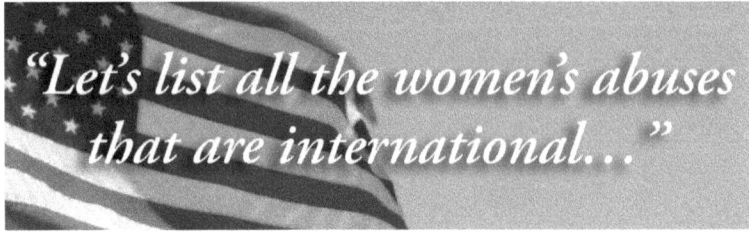

Let's list all the women's abuses that are international... then list the countries where they occur and publicize them in detail.

Makes our domestic concerns pale in comparison to the outrageous.

Cruelty to children... and cruelty to animals. Both are gigantic. We look away as if it is not our problem.

Extreme punishments go on in so many countries yet we look away. How about the use of a drill to gain information?? And some say sleep deprivation is worse? Nonsense. No different than poisoning an unborn child??

Protest, ready or not. Lazy solution. Let's just go do it and come together and it will be fun with like-believers. The like-believers cast the unbelievers as low-lifes. Yet we are all people endowed with the capability to do great things, if it weren't for being enabled and lazy.

The human being is a miracle. The human being is the source of love and caring and... power. Let's stop fighting each other and blaming the administration.

There are bigger wars to be fought abroad.

And if we keep on as we are we will become part of the caliphate that respects nothing.

Ready or not.

WWIII Has Begun

WWIII has begun.

The mushroom cloud of self-destruction has been dropped.

It will be an air burst at 10 feet.

Radiating all beings with protest cancers that will insure total disunity

Brother against brother. Mother against daughter… as the streets and crowds of like-minded consume individuality and peace. Drugs and politics and self-centric obsessions fire the all-consuming dissent.

We no longer honor our Flag or our heritage which is so noble and was sacrificed for.

In a vain attempt not to hurt the feelings of any people or gender we have become overburdened with stifling regulation and criticism. Free speech has been perverted into free everything. The voices of reason and good are crushed by the cacophony of the ill-informed. History is

"Free speech has been perverted into free everything."

no longer studied for lessons learned. Faith has become a concept to be wary of. All cultures have been declared innocent of wrongdoing. We blame ourselves for the troubles of the world. The only thing we worship is global warming.

We blame the police for not being perfectly sensitive.

We blame Washington for not addressing all our hypocrisy.

The poor cry foul.

The immature cry for legal pot.

Burn a car and it is celebrated.

The media has so much tabloid sensationalism that they can't keep up.

Every reporter is trying to be a star.

Every celebrity is trying not to sound vain.

Everyone is judging everyone.

There is no order or discipline.

Send in the troops.

WWIII has begun.

God help us.

Supreme Court

Courtship?

A lost art?

When you see that girl that you feel is the "one".... You start your impulsive strategy to win her over.... Hopefully ending in a "brief" kiss and submission...

Men tend to court all their lives. A dance of the roosters. It is like when we want anything...we try to figure out a way to get it until we know we can't, or are embarrassed at our obvious impulse. We don't want others to know about our courting behavior. Not realizing how obvious it is as all know the look.

When we don't want something we act like crybabies...

Hey... a woman looks just great in a little black dress. Agreed??

But a man??? No way unless he is a Judge... then they have to wear a large black robe. In both cases you get stared at and sometimes afraid....

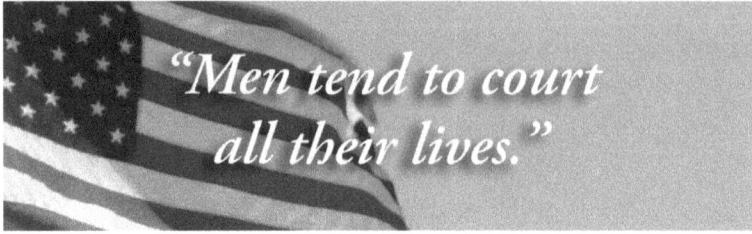
"Men tend to court
all their lives."

What is the biggest black robe of them all?? You guessed it... the judges on the Supreme Court!

They only debate and decide upon the most important issues of all. There really should be no dissention as the truth is the truth... and what is right should just be right... not left or right... What is good is good? What is Evil is Evil? Yet we want to excuse Evil with words of appeasement. Good is now being abused and criticized for not being sensitive. Go figure???

Maybe we really do need a Supreme Court. Why can't all the black robes get along and agree more often?... Why is there a shadow of politics in every case they review?

No authority is respected anymore. Lawyers are lined up to plead causes. The media injects its bias for all its viewers to consider.

How do we ever know anymore when an issue is presented without bias?

News people need to score points to be promoted....

Controversy means profits.

Oh Court Supreme… when are you going to rule on us?

Let's slow dance….

Foxy News

"She's a fox!

Gotta get her on the cover.

I'll go over and find out her story.

Looks are everything. See if you can get her cheap."

The fox winks. She knows the game. She has been news before.

She makes up a timely story and they run with it.

This fox knows exactly what she is doing. She actually told them the truth. It wasn't exciting enough so they enhanced it a little to sell it to their bosses. And the half-truth became a reality. You know the old saying..."The Whole Truth and Nothing but the Half Truth".

Fact checkers now have to find the fox for the truth except the fox is always one step ahead. She knows what they want. Anything that can be half-truthed easily.

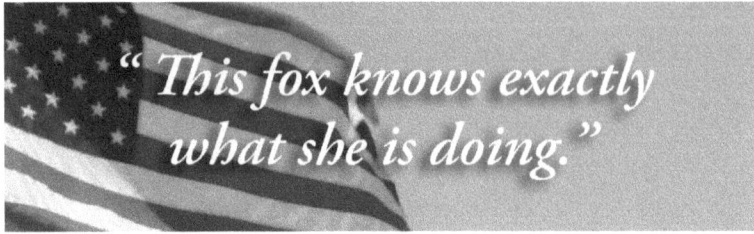

" This fox knows exactly what she is doing."

It takes a Fox to know the fox. Reporting the news is sacred ground. Human audiences are dependent upon the Truth to mold their lives correctly. Knowing the Truth that one can pass down is a sacred duty.

The Truth is no longer being passed on. It is so complicated and legally intricate. Old fashioned telling the truth from the heart is a lost art. Those that do get mocked and vilified.

We need a FOX to tell us the Truth. One who is not afraid of being caught telling the truth. One who is not afraid of being labelled shameful names.

It's Channel 5 or maybe Channel 428. You can find it. They still have the best talking heads. They have some foxes too.

Foxy News. It is much less biased than the competition. It is much more ridiculed than the competition.

Although recently there is some hope.

Let's make the News Great Again.

Why Die

Navy SEAL Chief William "Ryan" Owens just lost his life in a raid in Yemen. Did he die so we could live?

That is the biggest question of them all. Are you willing to die for something?

I think most would die for a family member. Like take a bullet for them.

Would you agree to die if you had a lot of money?

Can you make a list of people you would take a bullet for so they did not have to?

Or maybe agree to your own beheading so someone else would be spared?

Make a list of who you would and would not be willing to die for...

Does thinking about it seems kind of stupid and unnecessary? Why bother?

" *The greatest honor is to enlist in the military.* "

You should have someone on your list you would sacrifice your life for. Daughter? If you don't you are truly nobody.

To be somebody you must care for others, to serve them in some way. That is the most basic tenet of life. Yield to it and you will find excitement.

The greatest honor is to enlist in the military. Once the military owns you… it can send you anywhere in the world where anything can happen to you. You have agreed to serve your country, your nation, and all her citizens. One may end up in harm's way or dangerous surroundings.

You learn about rules, camaraderie, respect, patriotism.

You gain the new eyes of manhood.

You will look back at having loved your country.

You were trying to play a small part in protecting our freedom and love… Which needs more protection than ever….

Proud to serve. Shit happens. And you die. But not in vain if you know why. That you were serving in service to your country and her every family. That is classy.

You don't have to be a Navy SEAL to be cool. You just have to care by stopping Evil and falsehood and bullying and abuses in your own neighborhoods.

Die to self and you become someone special. Seize every moment to help or encourage.

Pray for our military, our President, and Ryan's family and friends.

Thank you for your service.

Flee Speech

"Flee" speech is the new name for "free" speech. Think about it.

Everyone has the right to "free" speech. That is one of the beautiful miracles of our democracy.

Except those who now wish to be heard have to yell louder over the majority. To get media attention they burn a car and smash a window. With total disregard to the rights of those they yell at and stone.

So good people must now flee at every protest. Not a Chinese pronunciation, "flee", but an act of safety.

Where is respect for human dignity? We should all be protecting our nation. Not dissenting it into chaos.

Shame was brought to UC Berkeley by herself pandering to bigoted dissent. No one who is invited to a university to present one of many views should fear for their safety. Universities are supposed to be the cathedrals of free speech, of human rights, and the truth found in history.

" So good people must now flee at every protest."

Students should know that it is an honor to be there to be exposed to the positive miracles of man's genius. There should be new courses of study considered. Here are a few: Values 101, Positivity 101, Compassion 101, Serving 101, Respect 101, Humility 101, Parenting 101, Providing 101, Accountability 101, Careers 101, Art 101, Math 101, Physics 101, Languages 101, Chemistry 101, Digital 101, etc. Now would not that be an exciting university???

For now should one flee a university?

Fleedom Rings?

Or make it better?

That would be true service.

Chicago Chicago

Chicago… Chicago…. It's a wonderful town.

Right on the lake is a perfect downtown.

It has grown so big and it has grown so good.

Frank Sinatra made it a city of romance. A perfect blending of what the heart of America is about.

What happened Charley Brown?

Torn with strife and bullets that confound all regulations. More murders, more crime, more blame.

The war-torn streets hold the tears of loss. Mothers bereft.

A magnet for drugs as the unhappiness within is still looking for answers.

Disunity is the work of the devil. Fear is his artificial sweetener.

Leaders soon learn they can't lead. Chicago… Chicago… they want to burn you down.

"Right on the lake is a perfect downtown."

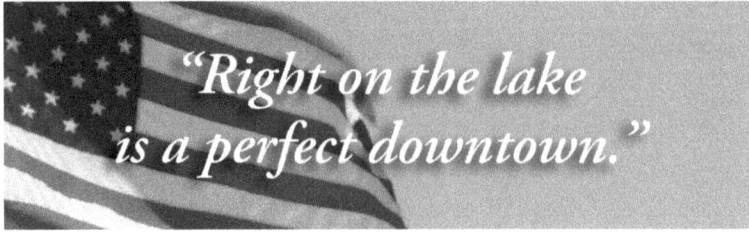

A mother's first scream is "hit the deck"… to get below the bullets. Soldiers know this.

Who forgives first when the body lies bleeding? Lawmakers meet and call for new laws. But, it seems to me, the laws needed are the oldest of laws. Fewer and fewer read that Book anymore. Carry that Book and you may be stoned.

I wish there were a $5,000 incentive for every youth to join the military. Therein is order and fairness and rules and discipline and respect.

Bring those gifts back to the streets.

Help Chicago get back into Frank's song.

Fifty Cents

Just give me 50 cents worth of the Truth...

No more. No less.

A perfect standoff. Nobody wins. It is a tie.

How do you break a tie? Shouting louder? Throw a rock?

Anger erupts when nobody wins. It's not the numbers on the outside, but the feeling of losing on the inside. Or should I say fear?

There is brooding chaos in our land of the free. Isolated we have not seen the horror of chaos. It's in the sands and destroyed lives of the black flag.

Part of our deep confusion comes from only knowing half of the truth. We are basing opinions and emotions on half of the story.

We have entrusted our future and our lives to our medias. From Facebook to Twitter to television to newspapers and tabloids....

"Anger erupts when nobody wins."

We consume half-truths with an occasional "aha!" when we think we have it figured out... the Truth ... that is....

We are great people who are more intelligent than given credit for.... If we know the Truth. We can make our own minds up. Bias in medias is a cancer distorting the very facts we need to survive. Being one who reports to the public is a sacred responsibility. No more noble a calling. No room for shading. Writing and choice of words is a sacred art. The truth must be respected and presented with integrity and humility. Then and only then is the reporter serving the public.

Not half the truth.

We deserve the "Whole Truth and nothing but the Truth, so help me God".

My Terms

I am going to do everything you ask as long as it is on my terms.

I am going to give you money as long as it is on my terms.

I am going to give you hope as long as it is on my terms.

The problem is that we all want everything on our own terms. With the onset of social media, texting, skype, tweeting, facebook… we all can be friends with people who agree with us. So we build up an ego reinforcing PAC (Personal Admiration Committee) that insures we are never wrong.

Our country has never been more divided and it is its own fault. Everybody is right. Everyone is yelling. Faces look red and veins blue.

In the end one person gets to call the shots. Or maybe one congress if it can unite and rule…..

"The problem is that we all want everything on our own terms."

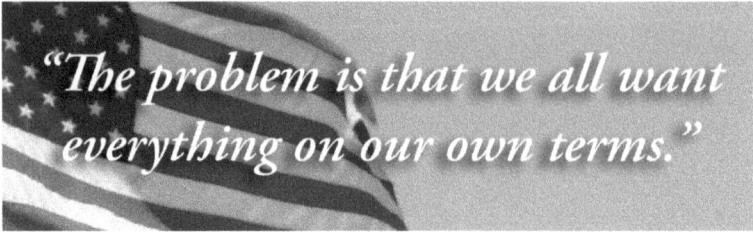

Do we remember when we were young and there were rules that sometimes worked? Things your mom or dad said to us that stuck? When their terms became our terms?? How long a list can we make? If we can't come up with 10 things then we are having more trouble than we can admit.

There is Evil and there is good. This is an important rule. We are supposed to do good to make the world better. We are supposed to help others to make the world better. Our terms can take us somewhere only if we put others first.

My terms are worthless otherwise.

Ten Commandments???

Freebees

Free the bees from their nest…

Or smoke them out and watch the frenzy.

Get too close and everyone gets stung.

It hurts.

It is scary.

Think about Congress as a bee hive.

The King with the blond hair rules.

Honey is made and industries of sweetness are fed.

Including the poor.

Everybody gets along with their stingers sheathed.

If they choose to be positive.

The King will address the hive tonight.

If they don't accept the truth, chaos and pain will reign.

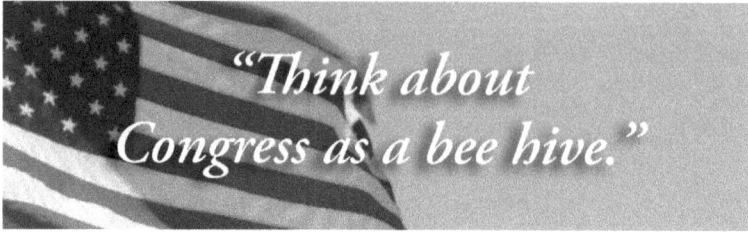

> *"Think about Congress as a bee hive."*

You see, everybody wants everything for free. When an applicant fills out a job form he/she asks about the freebees first: breaks, vacation, etc. If you don't have good freebees these days the young will look back down into their cell phones.

Maybe it is about time to realize that all the freebees are stinging us.

Maybe it is time to give rather than ask.

How can you kneel standing up?

Long Division

Before calculators and computers, mathematics was taught in all schools.

There were slide rules and there was this crazy math called "long division".

It was fun and ingenious. Fractions made real.

Kinda like factions?? Where everyone is divided and have their own strong interests.

From our Constitution's intent to… "United We Stand" to… "with Liberty and Justice for All" to… "One Nation under God, indivisible."

We no longer pledge allegiance to our flag in schools. We have become divided.

Last night President Trump pledged to the people he would no longer accept mediocrity for this country. The continental divide must find a way to be bridged.

"We no longer pledge allegiance to our flag in schools."

He appears to be willing to take all challenges head-on. He was talking from his heart. Ready for all the hits to come from the seated opposition.

Without unity we are destined to failure by our political bickering cancer.

Long division. Humph… We need a new math where everything ends up being a one. The world has no other leadership as great as ours. Tough calls are yet to be made. The math is not simple if it is long division.

I believe every citizen cares.

Let's text only the positive and become again a nation strong enough to frighten Evil and bring justice to those who mock our goodness.

Computer nation… it is time to attack from a united front!

Our grandkids deserve better...

Godspeed.

No Thanks

It wasn't until I got old that I finally realized how much a "thank you" meant.

Now my ears await the "thanks" back from the grandkids and friends when we give them something. A long time ago my in-laws gave me a lot and I don't remember thanking them. I didn't say "no thanks" but I did not say "thanks" either…

Maybe it's just with young people when their lives are so vibrant…and self-absorbed? "No thanks"… We have all been there. Today the subcultures of the "enabled" are growing at light speed. From cell phone affirmation to Youtube validation "thanks" are thrown out there. No thanks.

My wife always says…" thanks for asking". The waitress smiles. Her service is recognized. Kinda cool???

Some people have no reason to say "thanks". Maybe they are in the rubble of the Middle East or in the horror of the upper half of Korea… "Thanks for nothing" …..

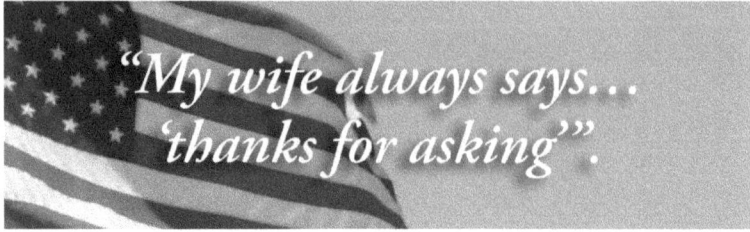

"My wife always says… 'thanks for asking'".

"No thanks" to our politicians for being so arrogant to not quickly decide for us. Shouting, denying, accusing….."No thanks".

There is always a solution to most everything. Common sense makes it obvious. Business sense makes it obvious. The truth makes it obvious.

"No thanks" for all the debates.

"No thanks" to congress.

"No thanks" for the intrusion of negativism in media.

Our Constitution made it clear. Where is the "thanks" for that?

The Bible made it all clear. Where is the "thanks" for that?

I apologize for not saying "thanks" all my life.

Mom and Dad…. "Thanks again."

You deserved better…

Looks Funny

Looks funny?

Sometimes your inner voice says that something looks funny…

I didn't say smells… just looks funny.

It's the first warning that something isn't right.

You keep it to yourself, but you keep thinking about it. Is it a danger or a lie? Something doesn't add up. Maybe a bigger war is brewing in the Middle-East….? Maybe there is too much agitation in the streets? Or maybe a friend said something that was not fair or maybe half true. Nothing to laugh at.

Something is funny in our nation. Good people are hesitant or afraid to say what they really feel. Their values are being trodden upon. They remain quiet as they fear being criticized.

Is this not a preface to a war? A war within nation and self…. It is about good versus Evil. We don't want to fight

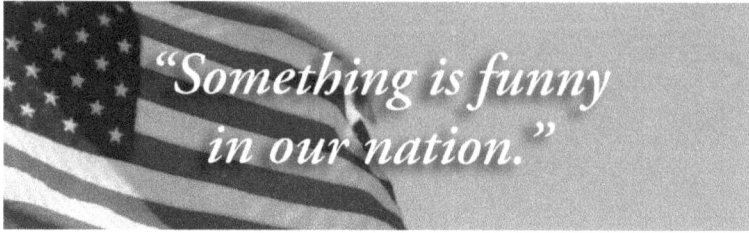

with words… the easy way is with bombs. But this is within our borders. Through our silence we have allowed the noise of the "liberated" to drown out common sense.

Religions have retreated from politics. Maybe it is time to rethink this paradigm?

Media is discrediting itself by not honoring the core values of our nation. The media has become their own pulpit while demanding the church's silence… Upside down?? Looks funny. Now you can laugh.

Let's have congress wear red wigs and blue wigs whenever they talk…

Now that would look funny! LOL

What should reporters wear?

Partisan Ship

We sailed the seven seas.

We discovered America.

We gave it a Constitution.

"United We Stand, Divided We Fall, So Help Me God".

Through fine print and litigation, we have neutered the intent of this famous and necessary document.

We have changed as a people. We are driven by wants and feelings. Nobody is the same. Our differences rule rather than bind. Free this and free that… Free expenses… Free insults. We are no longer classy. Bicker and bite. Besmirch and distort all in the name of freedom. We have sprayed our sanitizer on our ethos. We no longer believe in what we believe.

We have boarded the largest Titanic ever… I hear it is 40 miles long. Partisans in First Class. Believers in Second Class. This ship is going to sink. Ship of fools?

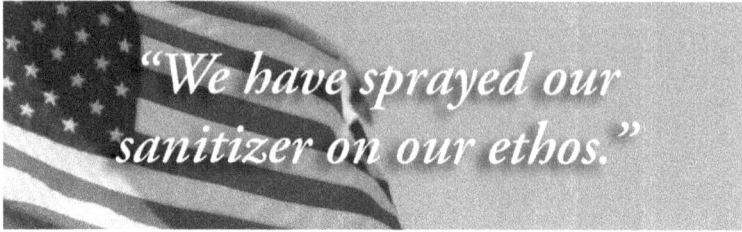

All the computers in the world will not be able to put our Partisan Ship back together again.

I suggest Celestial Navigation.

We all learned it in the Navy.

You look up to the stars.

As the Beatles sang… "Come Together…"

Where From?

I was getting some prescription eyeglasses.

They turn dark in the sun.

As she helped, she commented that everyone asks her all day "where are you from?"

It's like you were different, and everyone was telling you that all day.

Never happened to me. Hmmm...

We were looking eyeball to eyeball, up close.

She had a great personality and was professional...and kinda cool. So I said I am going to write a blog about "Where are you from?" Or... where are we all from? Some womb in a room.

These days we are paranoid about others being different. It has gotten so confusing as we are not supposed to have an identity that is different than the subject of-the-moment's

identity. We don't want to hurt feelings. This is what protests and stones thrown are all about.

How about we are all alike? That kind of neutralizes prejudice and judging? We all have different stories, parents, who had parents, who had no parents, who had parents.

Where are you from?

How does anybody every really answer that?

Genealogy and experiences are infinitely different. In that respect, we again are all alike.

There is so much more that can be accomplished if we just get over the "where are you from" trap.

I hate to bring God into it…but He knows. Talk to Him.

ASPCF

Animals have a tough go of it unless they are lucky enough to find decent and caring owners.

Not all are.

There is abuse and abandonment in the animal kingdom. Really bad with dogs and cats.

I can't imagine anyone being cruel to a Golden Retriever.

Thank God there is at least an ASPCA. But what about the rest of the world??

Why has man become so cruel to so many things? Cruel to it's poor. Cruel to it's sick. Cruel to its trees, cruel to its oceans, cruel to its women, cruel to its children. ASPCP, ASPCS, ASPCT, ASPCO, ASPCW, ASPCC….. you get it??

Sometimes we hide behind our organizations, thinking the problem is solved with some capital letters…

What is the difference between cruelty and abuse??

Nothing.

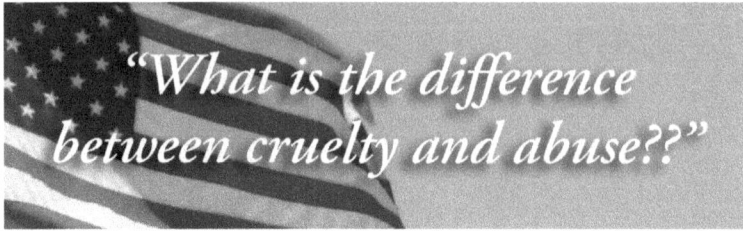

"What is the difference between cruelty and abuse??"

We have so many causes that are relatively ineffective. Offices that protest but never get to the source. It is man who is the problem. Blind and selfish decisions are made without remorse. If everyone said they would not abuse any longer…I mean everyone… then problem solved. There is a moral component to this kind of decision making. We don't want to be moral… it is too difficult. Maybe we need an ASPCM, American Society for the Prevention of Cruelty to Morals….??

When some of us were born into rough circumstances and didn't get the nurturing and love needed to be whole….. Were we weakened or made stronger??

Your story has its own uniqueness.

And lastly, after conception we become the unborn.

A cruelty choice is made.

Do you know what ASPCF stands for???

Slot Machine

"You are pulling my leg?"

"Are you really telling me the Truth?"

What does it take these days to find out the real truth?

We text and facebook looking for the truth. How do we know who is telling the truth? With no bias that is not admitted up front first? Isn't it important to know what you are dealing with? "Did he really say that???" How do we know without a video?

Wonder if politicians will use Skype? And maybe every politician should have a Go-Pro on his shoulder, lapel, or hat. Then maybe they would parse their over-worded responses more towards the truth. Maybe...

Now we all know the President uses social media and media to manage perception and understanding. It is so not traditionally presidential... hmmm... I bet this is just the beginning of a communication evolution that we don't

> *"We text and facebook looking for the truth."*

see coming.... Does not everyone have a right to address perceptions they disagree with?

And manners... politicians are not setting good examples. They are no longer independent champions of good and truth as they all worry about their perceptions back home.

We have created our own "Values Slot Machine" and the world is mesmerized.

Put a billion in the slot, pull the arm... ring a ding... bells... trumpets... and we have no clue what will come out.

So maybe it is time to stop gambling with the Truth.

There is a black book with gold edges......

Luvtrievers

Sometimes you throw the ball so far it is hard to find it.

We have done that with the Truth… thrown it too far… hmmm… hope it has a scent.

With so much protesting and half-truth we are losing grip on our game. We were champions of freedom and truth, not entitlement. Love is being twisted into self. Becoming a half-truth. Love is powerless if not helping others. That is full truth.

Everyone is not entitled to everything. Work entitles you to income. Which you can spend on any cause you wish. If there is no money in the Luv Bank, then you can't spend it or give it to a cause. It is simple math that we seem to be rejecting. Like no one ever went to school…???

Emotions are defying logic. Emotions are so compelling in their moment, but when the protest is over one has to sleep. Is one entitled to a place to sleep? Is one entitled to a car? To gas? To repairs? To a car wash? Can we agree on things we are not entitled to?

"Everyone is not entitled to everything."

There is not a nation that has entitlement figured out. They are in financial peril or pay their citizens $20.00 a month for their job in Cuba???

We Luv entitlements. We do not Luv paying for them. Who is the somebody else?? The rich? They have no money left...

Where is the love? I am owed something does not mean I love you.

I have said "If I only knew about Golden Retrievers before women??..."

Da Judge

"Here comes 'da judge"….. I forget who first said this… In some comedy show??

None "such" happening yet… In fact the confirmation hearings are just plain torture comedy.

What is a judge supposed to do? Isn't it to make sure that Truth prevails. That the Constitution is protected? Can't get more simple than that!!

Then there is "judge not lest ye be judged"… What in the world does that mean? Seems like this "judge" word is meant to be pretty important.

Except these days if you judge (aka… assess) someone you are guilty of some crime.

How in the world are we supposed to have anyone making decisions about us??!

Aha… we have the Supreme Court… I get it… the supreme judges… Like God with a black robe.

"Here comes 'da judge"....

We get to confirm whether this person is worthy of being God. We get to judge God.

What a mess we have created.

This current applicant looks like a pretty clean and independent soul. Let's get on with our lives; vote him in because we can't do any better anyway. We have so many more important issues to judge.... Like women's and children's abuse for starters... and the heck with all this corporate appeal nonsense... fine print be damned...

"Here comes 'da judge".....

Just A Guy

"I'm just a guy" is thought millions of times a day in private.

Don't blame me..."I'm just a guy".

What does it take to be a guy? Well, first there is an anatomy issue. That's pretty black and white, though in some quarters... debatable....

Assuming it is just your normal Joe, just a guy... and just a good guy. Being a bad guy is a waste of your time and potential. It is so stupid. Bad guys are stupid.

Most girls want a good guy. It can't be avoided. We exist for one another. A biological, social, and spiritual reality. A guy who loves a girl is acting with cosmic validation. It is natural and beautiful. Guys and girls in love is innocence and honesty and humility and truth. It is the life force that sustains life. If you are stupid then you can have any differing opinion you want.

"Bad guys are stupid."

Guys who are just guys like cars and sports and work and being fathers and husbands. Teaching a kid things you know that are good for kids is a beautiful thing to be proud of. Teaching them what good and Evil means... is an honor if you seize it. Helping your wife travel her tortuous road and being there at the end is what you are supposed to do.

It ain't easy.

It ain't easy being just a guy.

Guilt Edges

If you are honest with yourself there are so many things to feel guilty about.

In fact, guilt is a healthy thing.

It means you are being honest with yourself.

Carrying deeply protected private feelings of guilt over something you did is natural.

Hiding from them will invisibly eat at your soul. False confidence will cover it up as long as possible. There are very few people who have not earned guilt. Behind all the smiley faces is usually something being hidden.

Of course there is big guilt… and there is small guilt… Small is like when you don't say hello when you could have. You know you could have… and you get to experience your tiny moment of guilt. But one thing leads to another…

No matter how much guilt you are carrying, look for every possible good thing you can do every moment of every day.

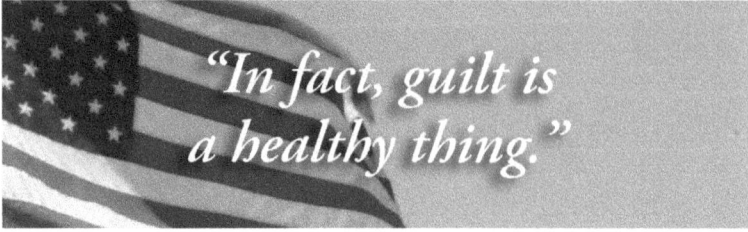

> *"In fact, guilt is a healthy thing."*

That will make you stronger for sure and put your guilt in a better place until you are ready to admit it out loud to someone.

Forgiveness is something you can give yourself... That's a little heavy. Think about it for a while.

There is an old Book about forgiveness...

It has gilt edges...

Widowmaker

Something hasn't been right for a while.

A gnawing feeling of mortality.

And then I was on a Caribbean beach every day. Walking from the water 15 yards on soft sand I could barely make it to the chair. A dizziness?? Ignored it. It's been going on for a good while. Flew home and was given a "procedure" to install my 4th stent in a new dedicated operating room right out of a science fiction movie. A monitor, 4 feet by 5 feet, was positioned just inches from me where my doctor focused his skills. It led him to my "Widowmaker" Artery. Google it.

This is the arterial junction between the right and the left main heart arteries. I had 80% Blockage. Heart attack territory.

The right and the left arteries must be able to do their jobs. In me they couldn't.

> ## *"The right and the left arteries must be able to do their jobs."*

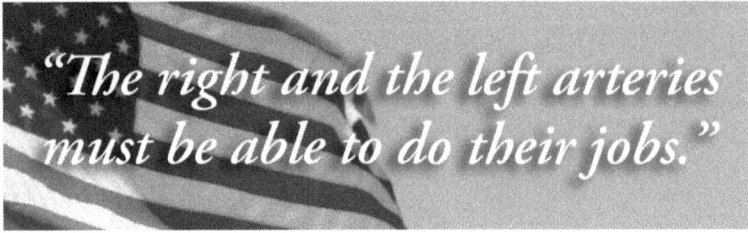

It seems that in our nation we have a similar situation. Surgery and change look necessary. We have a surgeon that nobody likes the looks of. He's different. But if he can't operate…??

The President is in charge of the heart of the nation. Congress is the Widowmaker if the left and right become dysfunctional. Democrats and Republicans are not acting in our country's best interests, just their own. Politics is clogging our arteries. Hello? Invisible corruption is rampant. Coats and ties try to suggest maturity and wisdom.

In 1776 hearts came together to enshrine equality in our greatest of all nations.

The world looks up to us for hope and Truth.

The Statue of Liberty is becoming a widow.

What can we do Charlie Brown?

Bomb

Do you know the smell of C4?

Is bomb a noun or a verb?

Does a bomb have a mother?

Broadway shows bomb.

Relationships bomb.

Countries bomb.

Each other.

Sometimes there is no other answer...

Too many mosquitos?? Bomb...

"Bombs away" saved civilization in the '40's.... depending upon your bias. Your bias would be non-existent or irrelevant if we had lost. Who loses? The dropper or the dropped on?

Maybe the same hold for words. Some hurt. Some are necessary. Some scar. Some heal. Your choice which to be....

"Why are bombs needed?"

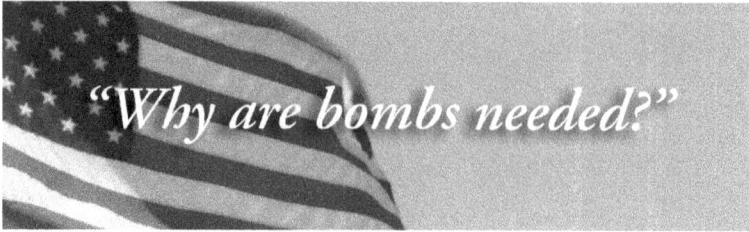

Asia is so pretty… Lotus blossoms and all….

The Middle East needs a bomb. There is no greenery anyway.

Korea needs a bomb. Who goes first?

Why are bombs needed? I don't think we know until after they are used…. Then debate and accusation reign. Victory means the loss of 100s of thousands of lives for the loser. Just to get 100 bad guys.

I am sorry, but bad guys are stupid and to whom life holds little value other than their own. We are not bad guys. To say we are makes you stupid. That's my opinion protected by the vanishing First Amendment…

Korea should be one country. Your choice as to which.

Sin is a bomb. Ask Adam.

Irrelevent

How important is the irrelevant?

Crazy question?

First... one has to know what is important.

The older we get the wiser we supposedly get... hmm...

But who determines what is wise? If it were left to us we can be sure some of our beliefs were backasswards. And Mr. Murphy will hopefully set us straight.

The political discourse these days... if you want to dignify it as such is disgusting. No more respect for any institution or person. Manners out the window. What is relevant is mocked. Hoods are worn to hide identity. Shame on them. Cowards to their belief.

Life is a journey to find the relevant. To find what you can believe in. To find Truth that transcends folly. From poverty to wealth, from pain to joy, from aloneness to family. There is ultimately just one destination that most spend their lives trying to avoid.

*"Life is a journey
to find the relevant."*

Deep in your heart lies the Truth. It is an onion to be peeled. You are an onion to be peeled. Eyes will water as real tears roll down your real cheeks.

Smiles will become genuine. Evil will be immediately recognized and attacked. Armies of good and compassion will fight as nobly as they can to protect what is relevant.

What is relevant is one man.

Each of us.

And... one born in a manger.

Donkey Tale

How can you tell which is a donkey and which is an ass?

It gets more complicated when you know the facts.

The donkey is a descendent of the African wild ass.

There is a dumb stubbornness image kinda associated with them. Then there is what task to assign to them. It ends up being the load bearer of infinite weight on the trudge from valley to mountain. I am not going to get political.... Domestically at least...

A donkey's tail is not very attractive, nor is the plant named after it. Giving no direction it just hangs off the ass. Usually that is all the donkey sees... the ass in front of him as they climb the trails. There is no way to know where it is going. A lot of people are like that ... they just follow the asses.

If you look at earth from space you can see borders and countries where there are more asses than necessary. And throngs of numbed humans following asses either in fear or indoctrination. If something isn't done ...asses could

"How can you tell which is a donkey and which is an ass?"

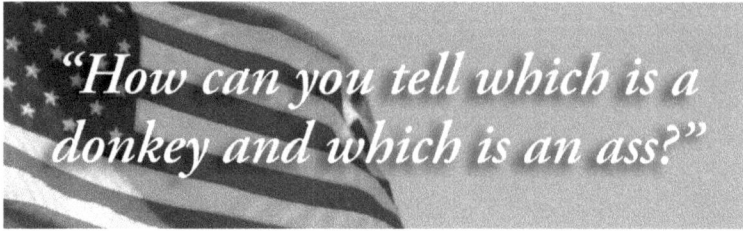

rule the earth. They are ruling many countries. Just ask the Secretary of State.

There are asses in political parties…. There are asses in media …. There are asses in protests.

There are asses everywhere and we all are afraid to call an ass… an ass. We are afraid of our own asses.

Asses beware, it is time that you got wiped…… out.

That is the tale of the donkey.

Eyes On

I see it.

Index and forefinger in front of your eyes.

In confirmation that you have found what you wanted.

Your buddy nods.

The moment of Truth.

Few will ever get to experience such a moment... or will they? There are so many things in life that are important to get close to. It is arrogance to think you can do it alone. Someone has to care about you to make the journey to that moment. That moment when you have to decide what is good and what is bad. I like the word Evil better. Evil must be dealt with before good can do its miracles.

There are people who quietly fight Evil every day both in the cammo uniform and in black and white. Black and white.... Hmmm that is where all our confusion is, settling on what is black and what is white. Nuns in a convent wrestle with good and Evil every day in prayer. In their own

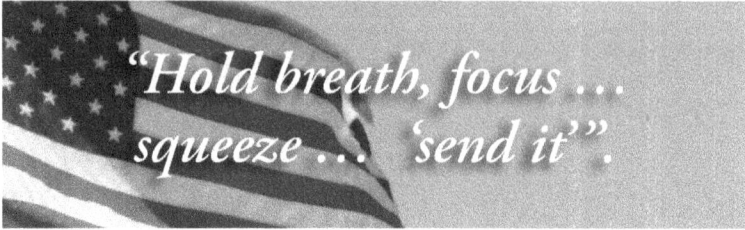

"Hold breath, focus … squeeze … 'send it'".

way they are at war too… Fighting injustice and unfairness. Not sure I want to be on their battlefield…. I think cammo is better… then Mister Evil can't see you until it is too late.

"Eyes on". Hold breath, focus… squeeze… "send it".

Too many have given up the will to fight. Our culture panders to feelings. Our youth have become soft while avoiding knowledge by giving themselves to the false affirmations of social networking. Heads down… not on real targets.

Media is celebrating itself. They no longer point us to Truth. It is going to be harder for all to distinguish right from wrong.

Are there "eyes on" our nation?

Is there a trigger soon to be pulled by the wrong people?

Pray harder Sisters, you may be all we have left…. Oops, I mean right.

None of This

"I will have none of this"....

My mother once said to me.

Maybe it was when I said my first bad word. I think she used this expression more than once over the years.

I think parents are saying this less these days for fear of being reported on .... LOL.

I think it happens in public schools. Teachers can be reported on by students.... What insanity....Even our nation and politicians have had to compromise when someone else comes on strong. Wiggle room is necessary to avoid decisiveness.

If we don't learn how to say no again, then we continue down the slippery slope of indecision and eradicate all traditional values.

To make "none of this" have meaning, action must be more than a speech.

"If we don't learn how to say no again".

Recently our Secretary of State is saying we will no longer put up with crimes against humanity. "We will have none of this." A powerful statement with far reaching implications if meant... if backed up with action.

I was writing on the fringe recently and got called to task by a friend.

Was it a student protesting?

Or was it a teacher saying No... "I will have none of this"....

Stopped me in my tracks.

She is a Nun.

Coat and Tie

There were posters of candidates in a coat and tie smiling back at you as you drove by.

This was in an island nation.

Except that this was the only time they wore their coat and tie except for weddings and funerals.

Somehow, the coat and tie makes one seem important, mature, and honest.

We love men in coats and ties. They are all over Washington like ants. Some of them say really stupid, biased things. It is often hard to discern the truth as they speak into the camera 3 feet from them. Some look good on camera, with God given smiles. A smile really goes good with a coat and tie.

Funny how at a funeral everyone wears white shirts and black ties.... And maybe a black suit. Does that mean that at death we finally know what is black and white? That life is better if we know the difference? Between good and Evil?

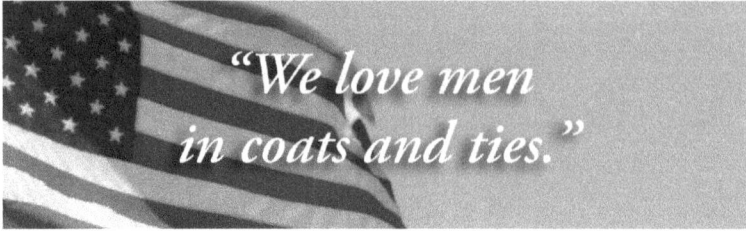

"We love men in coats and ties."

Why do we avoid confronting it? Sometimes hiding behind our coats and ties?

Celebrities love wearing black shirts with black ties…and black suits. They love black… Is it because it makes you look thinner? We look up to them and they know so little. They, like politicians have these important positions on important subjects that aren't important.

Oops, I am getting started. Tuxedos?? Penguins waddling around following each other?

I wonder if there is an instruction book that is Black and White???

Global Felony

Usually punishable by imprisonment for more than one year or by death.

Every state has their own take on what is a felony with a judge determining the severity of the punishment. Real punishment gives the word "felony" meaning. A felony is a serious crime.

The problem is that Evil *actually* exists. I contend that it is a felony to not admit the existence of Evil. If Evil exists then it must be confronted. Anything that is not good is probably Evil… not bad… but Evil.

Crimes against humanity are infinite… child abuse, women's abuse, torture, poverty, lying, drugs, hunger, and on and on and on. This is EVIL. Not social conditions. Where are the protesters??

Our world is boiling with slaughter and indifference to victims. Shame on those who make global warming their #1 priority. We may not have a world in a year if North Korea

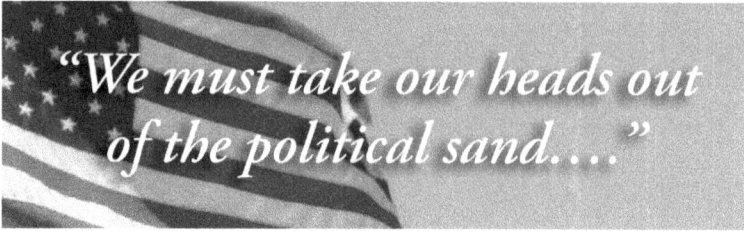

and others are rationalized away and not confronted. Evil has to be confronted. We must take our heads out of the political sand....

Global warming is not a felony yet. Awareness and education can solve it ... It won't kill us for 1,000 years if we do nothing.

WWII did exist. WWI did exist. The facts are horrific. Students today have no clue as to these atrocities. Much less to the real ones today. Where is the media?... The needed reporters?

How can we lead when all we do is criticize ourselves?

Crimes against humanity need to be punished.

It is our felony not to do so.

Is Real

Hello millennials!

History is real. It is there for you to Google in addition to your faces.

The street interviewer today paints a frightening portrait of man's growing ignorance. America has become so isolated and safe that it considers Evil non-existent, poverty being taken care of by the United Nations, and atrocity distant news from distant worlds. And to add insult to injury politicians and reporters porridge it into easy to swallow diversions. All sponsored by mind tingling commercials.

Good things get 15% of the news, weather 15%, celebrities 10%, and negative news 60%.

What is real? What can you judge Truth by?

Israel is for real. Do you think Israel is misspelled? Her circumstances are perilous and they have to stand firm every day. Are they a model for what is Real? They have difficult borders and walls. They retaliate with force when

threatened. How can they have survived with such hostile and Evil neighbors all these years??

They should be dead. They have no oceans to allow appeasement and vacillation. Interview citizens in the streets there and you won't find the blind ignorance found in ours.

In fact, real information is controlled and edited in most all the non-democratic nations. From Russia, the Middle-East, China, North Korea, Iran, Africa….. you could go on and on. Why are these places so misguided, so Evil? Not the people, but those who govern.

This cannot be Real. On the streets of Manhattan reality does not exist.

Schools no longer teach reality, just political correctness mindful that you can report on any form of authority at any time.

Israel Is Real.

Flag and Cross

Our nation was founded on tolerating the intolerant.

Now we are intolerant of what we stood for.

Our nation succeeded this far on her traditional values and patriotism.

Patriotism??

Is that not where small flags are shown on headstones in Arlington National Cemetery?

Where young lives have been sacrificed to insure intolerance does not rule??

Our public schools once were instrumental in forging young people with values and manners and respect.

Today they foment ignorance and disrespect. History is being twisted to suit the bias of the politically correct. Feelings rule.

Since when is our Flag not saluted or respected or shown? It is being derided as a symbol of the right. As if right was

"Since when is our Flag not saluted or respected or shown?"

wrong?? Give me a break. Teachers now look the other way and encourage the expansion of this bias.

Any young girl who wears her family-given small gold Cross is quietly mocked.

Christianity forged this nation.

Every teacher owes their job to it.

2,000 years ago the birth of Christianity changed the human race forever.

The forces trying to discredit it are massive and violent.

Enough is enough.

Ignorance abounds.

Religion has been forced to retreat while laughed at by the masses. It cowers too much.

This is no longer a debate.

Everyone else has come out of their closet.

Christians must do so now or lose the fight and nation and any hope of a decent future for all.

The Flag is waving at the RR Crossing. Stop what you are doing or be run over.

If you truly Love the Truth of Christ's Love then pray and act.

Church State

Churches are becoming labelled in our educational system as not politically correct... aka Evil.

Churches are where people congregate to learn about morals, morality, sin, forgiveness, and love... and Truth.

But don't be seen going into one these days. And definitely not if there are any cameras around. Maybe all Christians should wear body cameras like the police? Then we can catch them in the act of spreading their fake stuff.

I guess this gets the Middle-Eastern religions off the hook because we would not want to offend them by mandating body cameras on them. For all they do is good and sensitive acts.

So what is a church state?

Maybe we should have just one state for Christians like Montana. It can have Christian sanctuary cities where you can feel safe as an undocumented Christian. If they

"So what is a church state?"

all wouldn't fit, then add Idaho and Wyoming.... That should suffice for this religious minority. Okay... state your church! LOL

Then there are countries with state religions, which usually means no religion is a religion. Look at all the hypocrisy around the world in countries which tolerate some but not others. Do they look like they are a better place to live in than the USA?

Of course, our confused nation became this great country based on freedom and tolerance... a weird Judeo-Christian concept that appears to no longer have merit in the media.

OK, I get it. You aren't safe in the USA. It is a tragedy why so many in the military gave their lives in vain.

It is time to move to a real church state.

Except there is nowhere better to live than in America.

That flag I served still means everything to me.

God bless America and help us through these times....

The Bottle

Everyone carries the bottle these days. It has even become a fashion accessory to be seen with and adorned. Holders and hangers abound with designs and personalization.

Yes, the plastic water bottle has over-arrived. It represents purity, which we aren't, and health, which we don't have... For if we were we wouldn't be listening to every product ad that promises a better life through purchasing filtered purities. It is amazing all humanity has not already become extinct. Only to be saved by plastic. Yippee!!

We have entered serious times. No, not those defined by cruelty and nuclear proliferation, but by global warming. One way or another we are done.

20,000 feet down in the Ryuku trench off Japan are plastic water bottles. From Antarctica to the Artic the oceans floors abound with plastic water bottles. There are floating garbage patches in every ocean… 14 Billion pounds of waste are dumped into our oceans every year.

> *"20,000 feet down in the Ryuku trench off Japan are plastic water bottles."*

So when I see the fashionistas and celebrities flouting their plastic…. Oops I mean bottles… I think of the oceans carrying away our laziness to the horizons.

Well, at least I refill my bottle from the tap. Nobody has died from tap water that I know. If it were so bad how did I live this long?? But this now makes me anti something. Once labeled these days you can't get the sticker off. Labels come with super glue and there will be some protest group protesting my right to drink tap water… if they can catch me.

Now don't get me started on sanitizers…

Without

Times have really changed.

There is so much more now that one can't live without.

If you had X-Ray vision and could see behind garage doors you would be hard put to find a car.

100 years ago you did not know what you were missing. We know now…

Maybe each of us can find out who we are if we list what we can't live without???

Money, house, car, big screen TV, internet, cell phone, friends, travel, good food, beer… go ahead add to your list until you know it is complete…. It may end up seeming fun, but probably shallow…

All our lives we are searching for something elusive…. We don't tell anyone as it is very private and there is no one to share your deepest doubts with. Who you can really, really trust.

"Let's empty the garage of all things..."

Ok, just for fun…. Let's empty the garage of all things… a blank slate… what can we fill it with?

Can non-things be more important??

How about Love, Truth, Compassion, Sincerity, Humility, Honesty, Patriotism, Respect….? Add some more of your own.

It's so funny, but you can find all these in one Book.

And Someone you can really, really trust…

If I had to give up one garage it wouldn't be this one.

And there still is room for a car.

Enough

Yes Dear, you have told me that 5 times.

Enough.

Politicians say the same thing in 20 different ways into 20 different cameras. They just change their ties once in a while.

Reporters report on their same questions ad nauseam. No longer do they say "sir" before they ask a question.... And why does their question take 2 minutes to ask in 10 different ways? They are not reporting, they are just repeating the obvious. And why is their "opinion" more expert than the expert's? Enough.

Enough with no respect.

Enough with over explaining.

Enough with robo-voice prompts that do nothing but shield the company from live interaction.

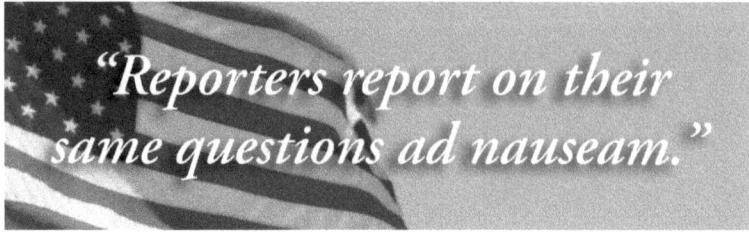

Enough with looking the other way to drug abuse… to child abuse… to women's abuse.

Enough with institutionalized political correctness. It is destroying our kids.

Enough…

Enough with terrorism and tyranny.

If someone wants to proliferate nuclear. Then nuke them economically. Then just nuke them.

We have brought this on ourselves by abrogating leadership.

Moral leadership is the only path. Otherwise what is the point of anything?

Who do you remember but the compassionate and moral?

We have become so intellectually arrogant to think morality is not essential.

Enough with this stupidity and those who are afraid to call a spade a spade.

Enough with not respecting our flag.

Enough with not respecting the Cross.

Enough is enough.

Carbon Dating

Carbon can't be all that bad.

It helps us determine how old anything is.

The oldest we can measure is about 50,000 years ago.

Of course, we all know that earth is 4.5 billion years old. That is a long time ago... before there were any religions and before we were capable of understanding anything. We gorillas had a long way to go.

Okay, carbon dating is helpful... but only to those of us who care about how old the person is we are dating. When we are dating we create a lot of CO_2... chasing each other around in cars... Intense carbon footprints. LOL.

Making wars does nothing to help but reduce the number of people who can breathe. Carbon emissions are going to kill us before we do? The way things look today we better get on with our inevitable wars so we won't be further distracted from the challenges of global warming. A couple of well-deserved nuclear wars should clear the way for

"Carbon emissions are going to kill us before we do?"

progress with our polar icecap crisis. Albeit with the tragic loss of trees and greenery that reprocess CO2.

Maybe we should revisit priorities. Reevaluate the importance of morality and unity? I bet that would do more for global emissions than all the protests and brutality. So much energy is wasted in discord.

A lot to think about unless you are smart and can put faith in miracles. And without faith we don't have much to hope for anyway.

Let's each consider becoming a moral solar panel… killing two birds with one stone.

Sun and Son…

Get it??

Global Cooling

I like it cold rather than hot.

I worry about global cooling.

It is going to preserve us all in ice… Cities and nations in the deep freeze.

Immobile and unable to fight any more.

As relationships between nations chill, big wars appear more imminent.

Nuclear war in North Korea seems to be a reasonable conclusion. The people there are cold already from deprivation and diminishment. Their hell is cold…. no Hope, no Truth.

Nuclear war leaves nothing behind but eternal cold after enormous heat.

Sad.

Global warming is not the threat.

"I worry about global cooling."

We are.

We are not protesting the Evil of terrorism and abuse.

Controlling carbon emissions is sound behavior and important.

But there are bigger priorities when you lift your head out of the nuclear sand.

Take a Chill.

Con Science

Right or wrong… I'm just doing it! And some impulse says you are right and you leap into the moment… into danger. Outcomes uncertain… You "just do it".

Remorse maybe… later… but not to act means you might own guilt….

We have glorified "conscience" as an explanation of moral urge. Someplace deep inside, some small voice hints at what is right and what is wrong…It's always been there, even as a child, but only as developed as the child. Then even as an adult, depending on your growth. I like what is right and don't like what is wrong. Good and bad. This heartfelt compass offers advice even when not asked.

These days morality gets a bum rap as it is labelled judgmental.

But one cannot shake one's conscience. Our name for our moral center. I call it a spirit of Truth, embodied in Love… We feel good being true to it.

This goes against all science. Science is the geometry of fact and analysis. From the study of galaxies to micro-organisms in our bodies. It is black and white. But is not good and Evil? Except no one dare say good and Evil is a science... maybe because we are further along with science than we are with good and Evil.

Con means against..... hmmm.... Con... science??

Morality is opposed to science?

The two are artfully brought together with the word 'conscience".

Something to think about.

If you have a conscience.....

You're Fired

"You're fired!"…..

I have heard that several times…

And guess what…

It was always for the best.

Thousands of CEO's and thousands of maintenance men have been fired for all kinds of reasons….

Many unfair… many because of political whispers from the insecure… get it?

What is all the fuss?

Come on… it will be replaced by the next crisis that is not a crisis…

Aren't soldiers' sacrifices more newsworthy?

Where is all the uproar about child abuse??

Single parent families??

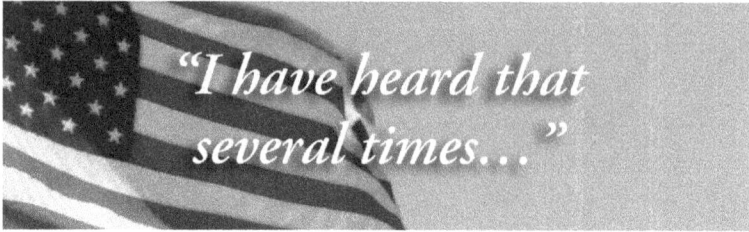

"*I have heard that several times…*"

The abuse of women in many other cultures is ignored.

Let's fire some of those leaders.

Getting fired hurts the pride…. But men get on with getting on…

Getting fired should get one fired up!

Point your gun to the heavens and get fired Up.

Con Sequence

Walk away unscathed.

That is what we all assume when some idea or scheme is figured out.

It is like we con ourselves into believing we are smarter than we are.

We plan the sequence of events believing we are inspired....

"Be true to yourself" rings in the deep recesses of our minds. Be honest and humble. And most of all find integrity... Then you will always scheme to get results that are good and unselfish and that make you stronger. Not to have to second guess one's self is a joy. Joy is the gift of integrity.

There are always consequences, always. Our challenge is to make the world better because of our choices. Our grandchildren need to know that we care about others in addition to them. They need to see the positive consequences of our decisions and feelings. So as we age we

> *"There are always consequences, always."*

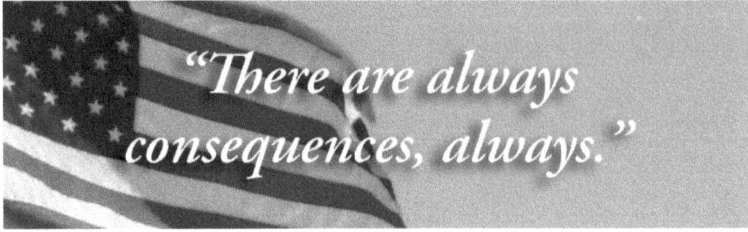

must charge ourselves with passing on Honesty, Humility, and Hope...

Young generations are hungry for Truth food.

They are hungry for the real consequences that make the joyful difference.

Teach them what has value.

Teach them.

Before you die.

Unfriended

Yesterday I was unfriended by someone I didn't know.

Or it could have been a person I thought was a friend.

How can you ever tell what someone really thinks about you?

To many it is to have as many friends on the internet as possible.

One's friend criteria is not the same as someone else's. And friends can hurt you more than non-friends. Maybe we should post our requirements for being a friend? But that could be embarrassing or hurt someone's feelings. Life today is all about not hurting feelings. You don't hurt mine, I don't hurt yours. But then how can you make any decisions before knowing the other person's feelings? Something to think about.... Just sayin'..... Confusing to me.

Walking in the woods or doing things alone is safer.

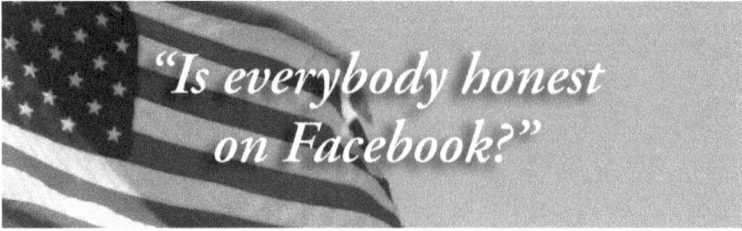

"Is everybody honest on Facebook?"

Is everybody honest on Facebook? I know it's fun… but also self-serving when not really honest… hmmm… Something to think about…. Just sayin'….

Be my friend so I can unfriend you? LOL. How do we unfriend Evil? It is much harder and more serious and ignored by most as it would take too much energy and risk hurting feelings.

There is so much good in social media if it is used to fight for Truth. But it has become self-indulgent and narcissistic.

I think I am going to unfriend social networking and go ride my electric wheelchair.

Just sayin'.

Bittertweet

Whisper whatever you want into my ear, but keep it to 140 characters.

I know it is hard to be concise, but those are the rules. You will not be allowed to over-express yourself with 141 characters. Isn't it funny that we can challenge and protest all the other rules in the world? Challenge the Constitution, Religion, Common Sense…. Lawyer up and take it to court. But not the length of your tweet my sweet tweetie. You have to follow Rule 140. Rules??? No rules we said??

Tweets can be good and tweets can be Evil. They can be flattering and they can be disrespectful. Nothing is sacred, just the 140 characters. They are the new 140 commandments… LOL

Or maybe this is a breakthrough? The first new rule of rules. Will congress approve? But… they have no jurisdiction… hmm…

It looks like we now get to set our own rules??

> *"Tweets can be good and tweets can be evil."*

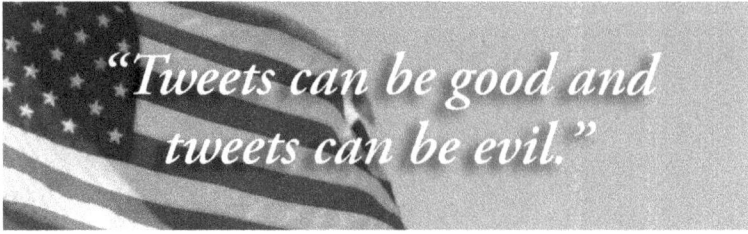

But!!! We don't like rules!!!

None are taught in schools.

Religion says there are rules?? Ridiculous.

They say He talks to the heart without characters.....

Maybe we all should just communicate heart to heart. About what matters... Dealing with Evil and helping others.

"Just do it".

That is less than 140 characters.

Hearts rule my tweetie....

Artificial Intelligence

Now your car can park itself.

Are we supposed to give it some rights as it now has a brain?

Feelings?

Artificial intelligence is being integrated into almost everything we have. Just wait and see.

Cognitive computing.

All human opinion is now suspect.... And subject to computer cognitive evaluation. Huuhh??

Hey... we need to build a wall between us and 'dem computers.

Roombas that protect us will be everywhere. Would you believe there are over 100 models as we speak?

What the heck is intelligence? I think it is about knowing the difference between right and wrong.... Good and EVIL. We are no longer able to distinguish between the two.

"What the heck is intelligence?"

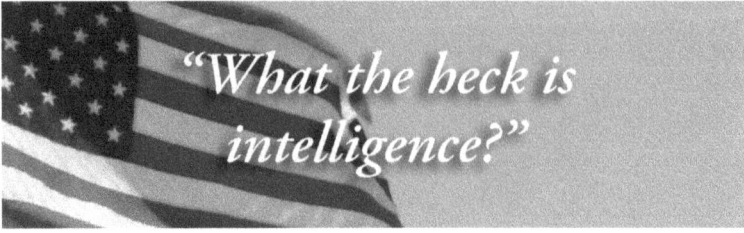

It is not politically correct to judge Evil, as the perpetrators have their stories and feelings that eventually mitigate responsibility. Whoa….. Slam on the brakes….. Let's stop and see where we are. The answer is looking down into our cellphones which are now manipulating our every thought.

I check my artificial intelligence sources on my social networks to make sure I fit in. I am becoming the robot.

It sure looks that way in the restaurants. Everyone is faking looking at the menu while they remain glued to their little screens.

Robots on Facebook….

Twitter-on lost souls.

Magic

Magic is our term to label something we can't explain.

It is unexpected and usually harmless.

A magician's cape that hides the live rabbit. The swords that go through the magician's body but don't. Sleight of hand is a form of art that brings smiles of amazement to all ages.

We are going through very difficult times. It seems as if Evil and chaos are even more out of control. It will take a real magician to bring smiles back.

Except that we all have our own capes. Given to us at birth. Each of us is so unique. There are people who are waiting for us. We love bringing smiles to children. Isn't a child's laugh the best??

The last magician magic I saw was at a Navy reunion. There was this teammate Chuck, the snare man, who did his magic in the water a long time ago, who now did his magic with cards and sleight of hand walking around

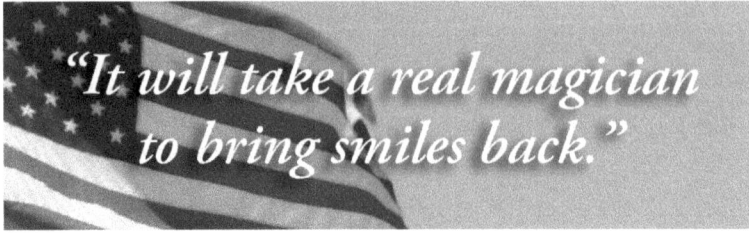

from table to table. It was such clean fun. He was an artist, painting smiles on faces so wanting.

When you do things for others you too are a magician.

To them, to see that someone cares makes smiles come back. You feel private pride deep within. Magic, absolute magic.

We are all here on earth to make others smile. If one gets too caught up in self or all the plentiful distractions, one will never seize the moment that could have been.

These moments are seen from the heart if it is free to see.......

2,000 years ago magic started.

Anti-Social Media

Social media has captivated the attention and time of most of the world. Anyone who can get a cell phone or computer are CAPTIVATED! (Me too.)

Wait...the word may be Captive. Are we all captive of it? Does this not infer there should be an Escape plan?? Nobody wants to be a captive... Hmmm...??

Social means being friendly and social... I thought.... Ways to make friends and be a meaningful part of more lives. Being friendly to more people makes one feel good. It was a smash success. Friending someone in Europe or Asia now made easy...

Groups of like minds now form new group think. Except for some reason, they are becoming attack entities, packs of word wolves.... Hungry for targets....

Politics. The battlefield of the slighted and entitled. Normal people go about their lives, go to work, go on vacation, go to church... keeping their views to themselves.

> ## "Social means being friendly and social."

Except when the television is turned on…

Then we see "enlightened" reporters, expert at nothing, clamor for attention with undisciplined innuendo and insult.

Anti-social media has been born. And it is turning society upside down. Conservatives withdraw… perplexed.

Morality is now relative. The most recent tweet is a headline. Infinite texting becomes the mortar of half-truth. Our traditional social foundation is under attack by anti-social media.

Hands need to be shaken, not phones.

Looks like you can't have Peace and Love without War….

The Quarter

What has more value?

A million dollars or a quarter?

Which buys you more happiness?

The quarter can if it is your last and you give it to someone in need.

This trumps the million every time.

Sometimes life can be very unfair. Sometimes life can be very painful.

Sometimes some decide to check out early on their own. Those are tragic, private stories.

Sometimes all we choose to remember is the bad that we did. One will never forget the first bad thing. Like a child stealing a quarter. Still remembered silently on one's death bed. The guilt carried all one's life.

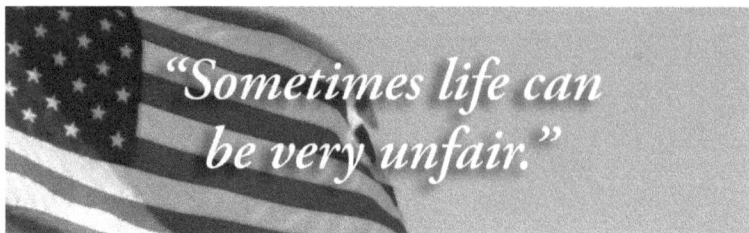
"Sometimes life can be very unfair."

Many try different streets to outdistance the bad one has done, the hurt caused to others. Streets of arrogance, drugs, or denial.

There ultimately are two streets left. Death or Truth.

Truth comes from accepting your weakness and asking forgiveness.

Truth comes from learning that bad is not good.

That good is helping others, no strings attached.

Uniqueness is forged through adversity. It is not a gift.

You do not become who you were meant to be without pain and private suffering.

I know a man who never has forgotten the 25 cents he took when a child. Haunting him throughout the years and nights.

I, a complete stranger, said "I forgive you". That he was special in his remorse. That his new life will be brighter as he had found humility and focus. His work shows it.

No compromise any more.

Maybe I should put a ribbon on a quarter and pin it to his overall's pocket?

In Security

Every one of us will do anything to feel secure.

Husbands are meant to protect the family. They are to provide security.

Women can't be women if they don't feel secure.

We need money to feel secure.

We need our car to feel secure...

Often we spend more money to make our car look expensive which is supposed to signal we are secure.... That we have status... But it does the exact opposite.... Hmm?? True??

We try to hide our insecurities behind all kinds of pretense. We are never comfortable about our insecurity. A lot of acting is involved...

Lacking security one tends to deflect by criticizing others... deflecting attention from our own core. Insecurity creates negativity.

There is too much of a focus on the negative today. Look at all the networks. What are they afraid of? They have forgotten their role. Go through every news channel. They are fighting for attention. They are acting like insecure teenagers. They are turning our society upside down. They no longer teach good. Our schools no longer teach good. They are neutering the soul.

Insecurity must first be hyphenated (in-security), then finally made into two words... In Security.

It is through Love of others... It is through helping others that the Soul heals. One does not feel insecure when helping someone. One feels they are in the Right. They know it is right. They become who they were meant to be. They can stand up for good and fight the folly of the negative.

Die to self must come first to be "In Security".

Got It Covered

"Got it covered Dad".

All of a sudden this new phrase enters my world.

Is it about making the bed?

Is it about my car cover?

Car covers are really important as they protect and give longer life and appeal to our most prized possession other than self. Bet car cover companies could make a fortune if they made people covers. Fewer wrinkles. Weight control. Better sleeping.....

"Got it covered Dad".

Got to think about it... Have never seen it in literature and the TV that I watch. It is annoying that I have to learn vocabulary from younger generations and my children and.... Grandchildren...aghhh...

"No worries" drives me nuts. It is so stupid. That the person saying it is absolved of any responsibility or

"No worries" drives me nuts.

something. I wasn't worrying before that was said. Now I have to think about what the other person thought I might have been worrying about.

Maybe it is signaling that it is time for me to accept old age. I am always looking for the next chair. I can't run anymore after having run thousands of miles…

The top of the stairs is no longer looked forward to.

Petting the dogs is.

Hallmark Channel is exciting.

I love my polar fleece at night.

"Got it covered, Dad."

"No worries."

Patriotic Duty

It is my patriotic duty to inform you that we finally have
screwed
it all up.

"Freedom of Patriotism" is now derided as unpatriotic.
Go figure?? What in the hell is going on?? The dissenters
are labeling everything patriotic as conservative right
extremism. I never asked to become an extremist. How do
they have the right to make up labels and hurl them like
biological grenades? I want to throw up.

Rules on Flag use. Taking down the morning "I Pledge
Allegiance" is a stupid sin. Like teaching respect and love
for your amazing democratic nation is Evil??? Respect for
nothing is taught in schools other than for the sensitivities
of minorities. What about my genuine sensitivities??

Disrespect my sensitivities and you have war. Don't
underestimate the sincerity of the anger of the veteran.

We all feel the swamp needs to look in the mirror.

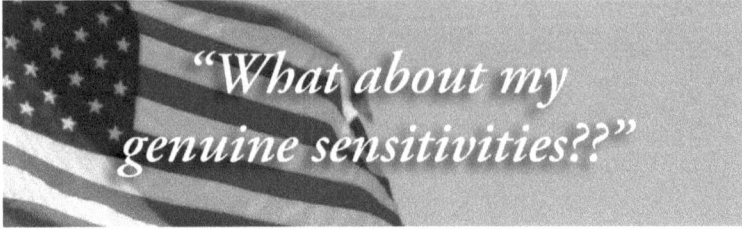

Paper pushing has become their cancer.

Talking to the camera has become their cancer.

Their patriotic duty is to give the governing back to the people.

Titles and salaries and benefits need to be cut.

They should not be paid more than us.

Now to the subject they can't handle at all. God.

It is our Patriotic duty to not take God out of our history, off our buildings, and from our monuments. Let Arlington ring with a warning to love thy country as before. To stop the bureaucratic rape and pillage of her history.

We are free because of God. God bless America.

Sophisticated Arrogance

Hallowed be thy network.

May thy editor's will be done.

Make the truth be obscure so it will be a hell of a lot more fun… For some….

Reputations dangle in the wind. As the ignorant and biased laugh and laugh and diminish their worth.

Sadly taking us all down with them.

Everything is fake except death.

Remember the Lone Ranger? Where is he when we need him? Can't he just jump off the comic book page and ride into Washington and defend the drainers of the swamp??

Reporters used to be like priests. They used to be beyond reproach. Seekers of the Truth. Exposers of injustice. One couldn't wait to read the newspaper front page to know that brave good men were subduing evil. That the milk was being delivered. LOL.

"Reporters used to be like priests."

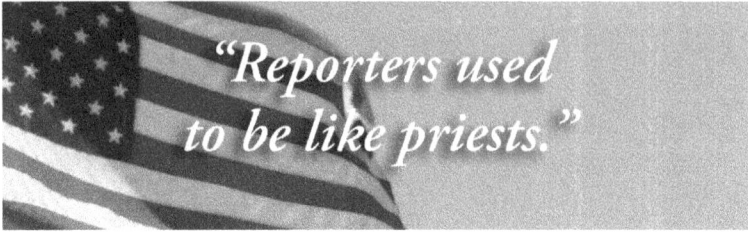

Celebrities who deal in the fake will chime in from some distant island of arrogance. And still make it to the magazine covers!

Pundits are so arrogant with their self-assertive sophistication that they have no more value than a water slide with blue colored water. Whatever the heck that is? They go to college to get a degree in arrogant verbal self-immolation. Whatever that is?… LOL.

Experts in neutering religion.

Experts in making values seem biased.

Sophistication abounding with arrogance.

Where have all the newsmen gone??

Long time passing…

Eyeway Robbery

It's raining.

Some liken raindrops to tears....

Our beautiful nation is criticizing itself to death.

It is a time for tears... for those who have given up.... I repeat... for those who have given up. Or as a few of us know, rung the bell....

Regulations will mean fewer cars on the highway. Laws mean there will be less freedom of thought as more subjects are added to the avoid list. The highways of the mind will be regimented. Heads are already locked at a downward angle pursuing what little truth is left on the internet. Eyeway robbery?

Thoughts are being stopped and interrogated.

DUI. Driver under the influence of the subversive Truth. Whistleblowing is no longer effective.

"*Thoughts are being stopped and interrogated.*"

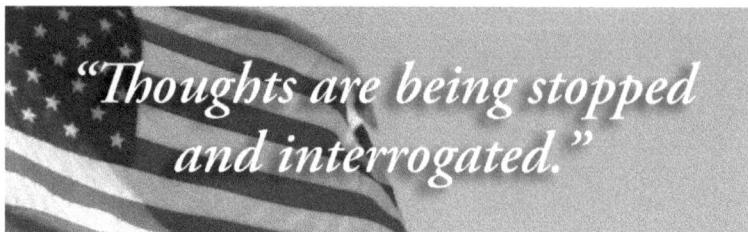

Everything the eye sees and the ears hear must be examined for validity. Is it real? Is it Right?

Is the gun pointed at you just verbal or is it metal? What is the difference if it can kill you?

A person who holds a gun is now labeled as disturbed and needing understanding and sensitivity training. The time it takes to ponder this could be your last breath.

Evil in the most subtle of forms is killing us.

The arguing in media is killing us.

However you define your front door, keep it locked.

And keep your Glock 19 nearby.

Deaf Hearings

He's testifying!! Shhh…

They are going to ask him so many questions.

It will take hours.

Agendas all over the place

Friends, enemies, observers with extensive portfolios of bias. The points are so fine that everybody is invisibly bleeding from the pricks…. "I repeat"… dithers one Senator. Serious faces inferring serious consequences.

The trick is to put fingers in your ears so you hear nothing. You just feel whatever is there. Anyway, we all know that these days feelings are more important than words.

Actually, no sound should be transmitted of the "hearings". Get it?? Just look at the faces and you can figure it all out. In 2 months, it will all end in one sentence. The public verdict.

Depending also on the color of your state… LOL

"They" act as if we are all deaf. As if we can't "get it" without their help. The guy driving the tractor in the corn field in Iowa can't hear a thing and he "gets it". The guy selling commercial real estate in St. Louis "gets it". The celebrity in Los Angeles proclaims he is "getting it" while totally deaf to the truth.

Global deafness is the next crisis that should be the next marquis event at the United Nations… and touted in see-through gowns at the Academy Awards.

Need a hearing aid??

There is a Black Book….

So Funny

Johnny Carson was so funny.

He'd tell a joke then laugh as much as you did.

There was so much humor in everyday simple things.

Laughter is good for the soul. It energizes optimism. You just feel good. Like love…. but different…

If you made fun of someone it was wholesome and all could laugh, including the target. All kinds of shows sprouted with humor at their core. Good times for all. We all were united in smiles. The next day you heard the sharing of laughter based on last night's shows. Hey… We had "I love Lucy" and Ricky Ricardo…. Silly vintage champagne for the soul. The grumpies even cracked a smile…

Somewhere along the way there was a train wreck. Our foundations of respect and reverence got buried by piles of self-serving nonsense. Our politics grew combative. Protecting your re-election drove your media interaction.

"Breaking news was breaking with the truth."

Statistics replaced eye contact. Banners and slogans defiled discourse. Blame became the game.

Breaking news was breaking with the truth.

Opinion and bias delighted editors. Unfair and unbalanced is now our norm. Nothing is funny. Late night humorists have unlocked their foul mouths and bigoted brows in a cacophony of derision and smugness.

Major networks and news sources are blindly feeding revolution.

At their own peril.

It is so funny that they are so blind.

Leaky Leaks

How did leaks become so polarizingly political so fast?

All it used to mean was that you were going to take one.

And when you got real old it became the new normal. At least they have product to control it...

Today everybody is leaking. But the worst leakers are the press. My gosh do they love going around sniffing for leaks. You know, that certain odor... LOL

They are adding leakinals to our bathrooms. Where leaks can be collected. Simultaneously catching DNA along the way for the NSA. "To leak or not to leak" is now the question. Kinda Shakespearean???

Of course we are finding that there are fake leaks. I don't know what that means....

You can leak red and you can leak blue depending on your state.

"*Today everybody is leaking.*"

Unknown sources close to the leaker validate credentials of the un-named expert.

Truth has become a shell game….. I promise to tell the Truth as long as you protect my First Amendment Anonymity Rights…or whatever…..

Las Vegas rules now apply in Washington. Everything is a roll of the dice. Who gets fired, who gets promoted, who is held accountable, and who the people really trust.

If you don't fit into the establishment you will be leaked on.

Now that is a pisser.

Poll Dancing

What a set of gams!

Spinning around that poll.

The phones ring asking you for your opinion.

Asking you in a computer voice to hold, a dancer will be with you shortly.

You hear accented voices in the background.

A guy asks you which dancer you are voting for. What characteristics do you admire?

Why give this information to this stranger? How do you know if there is bias in this pollster? The questions seem so stupid. This is not science. It's dancing words all going into a fake poll product that someone is paying millions for. How do you know it is true? Who are the people taking a pass on participating? How do you quantify them?

> ## *"A guy asks you which dancer you are voting for."*

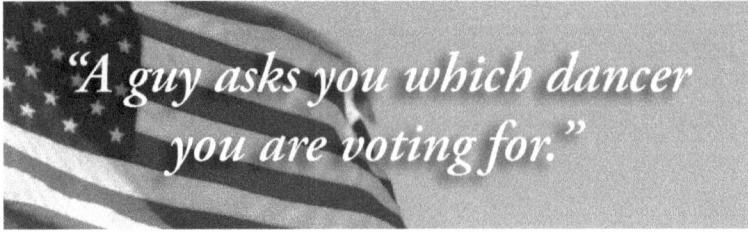

It is the Washington DC political shell game. Accusation and proclamation based on slippery poll moves. Winks and kisses. Expectations aroused....

The evening news amplifies the charade. Tones of certitude and importance roll from the anchor's pearly teeth. Impeccable suit, white shirt, and tie that never show the jeans...

Breaking news from certified poll dancers fill the headline banners and scream urgency. We rush to the kitchen during the commercial so as to not miss the next erotic spinning. If you close your eyes the gal looks terrific.

Open your eyes and the truth is never what it seems.

Congressional hearings continue their dance.... in circles....

Love those heels and stockings... wink, wink....

Databaseless

Marooned in a database for life.

Parts of me spread throughout cyberspace. I want them back. Life was good when nobody knew anything about me... They couldn't Google my name before they met me. They couldn't look at my Facebook history and make assumptions.

I want my privacy back. I am not a terrorist.

I am a nobody of bits in a computer cloud. My opinions are deduced from data. I am polled without a say.

I used to go out and play, but time is so precious as laptop and phone devour my day. I am too reachable by digital distraction that the kayak no longer gets wet. Sports are on big TVs with the refrigerator close by.

There are commercials for everything I want. How did they know that? Who are the "they"? I have never had a personal contact with any one of them".

> *"Parts of me spread throughout cyberspace."*

How do you look a man in the eye if it is only a camera lens?

Is there a database laxative?

I want to start over and open a chain of Database Purging Centers.

Serene music and smiles.

No forms to fill out.

We only deal in cash.

Opinionitis

There is a brain cancer spreading.

It is severe on the left side of the brain.

The right side really cannot function without the left.

You see, the left side is now full of negative opinions. Cerebral gossip taken to self-destructive levels. Incoherent noise that is not easy to translate.

The brain is made of grey matter and white matter. It cannot function without both. The right side is mired in righteousness... (Just making this up.) In any case you get the drift.

How come Advil sales are going up? Headaches.

Or drug abuse? And... all the other forms of abuse?

We just can't deal with all the opinions from all the experts. Advanced degrees flaunted as their weak assertions are made. Biased reporting is accepted as the new norm.

"There is a brain cancer spreading."

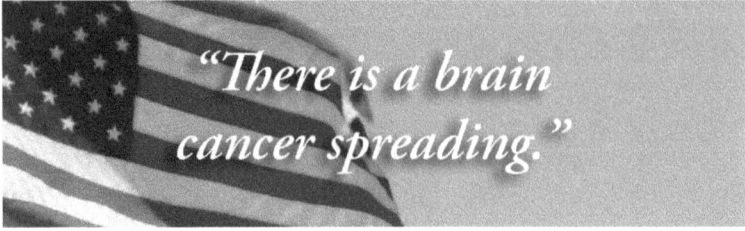

We turn off the TV a lot more.

It is safer for the young to do video games and the elderly (me) to now play "Las Vegas Slots" on my iPad. The evening news is incestuous gossip.

Opinions no longer come from informed facts, they are now driven by emotions. Like "I don't like that guy because his blonde hair is funny".... Except that men's hair is now over the top ridiculous anyway.

Opinionitis.

Yep... the beds in the cancer wards are filling up with people who have given too many opinions and who have listened to too many opinions.

What is right is wrong.

What is left is nothing.

Pelosification has set in.

What's your opinion?

Cruise Ship

Escape.

Why are we all trying to escape? From what? Ourselves? The world? The injustice?

Deep within something is not right. We don't feel in complete control. We resent it.

Enter a solution. The cruise ship.

Millions of people are going on these giant comfy ships and love it.

Now I love the ocean. Can gaze at it for hours…. And I got to know every aspect of it in the Navy. I have been there… She chose not to take my life.

Today cruise ships have water slides… Go figure. Restaurants, entertainment, bars, shopping… and lots of fellow landlubbers to party with. Most all rooms have windows with ocean views. And many with none. It doesn't matter. Fun is glamorized and the cruise ship has it all… plus sunrise and sunset….as you wish.

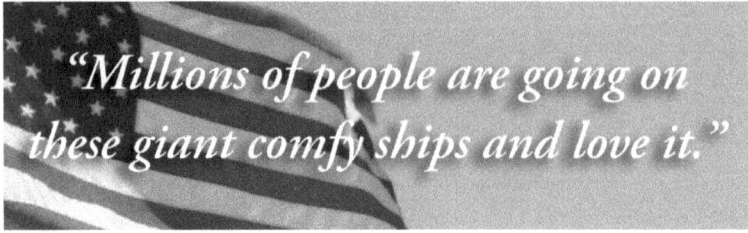

Is it really getting away? Escape? Anchoring in ports for a night or two. Offloading like cattle trying to race to the shopping or to the snorkel or dolphin bus? Parasailing, jet skiing, tours of all sorts. Organized paradise. Escape.

Your bed and cocoon are made and cleaned for your return. Guaranteed.

To a seagull 500 feet up it just looks like a fishbowl full of humans. Everybody walking around waiting to be fed. Happy and anxious for the next event.

There must be a root cause. Is it to reduce effort to a minimum???

Everything today tries to be convenient and alluring.

Safe, secure, and comfortable.

Like going to a carnival on a lazy-boy....

Tiny Church

Church is so mislabeled and criticized and scorned and rejected.

Something has to be the cause of all our unhappiness. So people who claim to know it all are the first mocked. Been going on since forever...

Somewhere, someone must have a handle on what is right and what is wrong. How do we find them? Are they poor or rich, Hispanic, Russian, Arab, American...??? YouTube?

Maybe if you look into the night skies and deep into the infinite galaxies, you will find a way to start your journey by accepting that you are beyond finite and unable to comprehend creation.

Then there is this little tug inside that some label conscience. Trying to pull you one way or another. It is often your last resort when all the experts fail.

Your conscience reveals the Truth.

> *"Church is so mislabeled and criticized and scorned and rejected."*

This is your church.

Talking to yourself is okay if you are searching for what is the right thing to do. You don't need tall steeples and ornate altars to search... until... you are ready to accept them as potential aids.

Of course, there is no God.... Unless you just believe of course. So try talking to Him as if He were real... just for kicks. Just for a week. See if any of your opinions are affected. Nobody has to know. You report to nobody but yourself.

You will have been in your own church for a week. Your Tiny Church.

You don't have to kneel, you don't have to pay, you don't have to pray.

Make my day.

Happy Hour

Pharrell Williams sings "Happy".

What is "happy" anyway?

We usually can tell from smiles and laughter. A release of involuntary genuineness.

We like being around people when they are natural.... And honest.

Then there is fake laughter where a person is trying to hide their insecurity, their truth.

There is also Evil laughter. It is not that cut and dried......

Bars promote "Happy Hours" where things don't cost as much. Go inside and feel the alcohol induced genuineness.

Happy hours can be found hiking, running, or playing sports. Happy for an hour can be found on Hallmark TV.

Happy hours can be found being honest with one's self. Listening carefully to that little voice in your heart directing you towards the right decision. You can smile

> *"Bars promote 'Happy Hours' where things don't cost as much."*

and even laugh when you see it and choose it. And as you execute that decision.

But the most real happy hour comes when you quietly help someone else. You know the glow. As you move on to your next opportunity you feel sublimely and privately happy for at least an hour, if not many more, if not for a lifetime.

There is nothing wrong with unspoken pride.

Look up and smile.

Thin Crust

He was a crusty old sort.

Weathered and opinionated.

There was one thing he would not budge on.

Thin crust pizza.

He'd had it in Little Italy in New York when he was young and just couldn't get it out of his mind.

A benchmark pizza, a great thin crispy crust that was chewy at the
same time.

Every piece was great… marinara, mozzarella, and pepperoni.

Cheese stretched a foot… What flavor and fun.

Over the years he found a few places that made his benchmark.

The biggest smile ever after the first piece.

"Once you know what 'good' is you chase it all your life."

Salt and decadence that was legal...

Once you know what "good" is you chase it all your life. Good food, good wine, good people, good acts, good love……

Then you start to figure out what makes things good.

You see that it is honesty, humility, compassion, unselfishness, perseverance... These "goods" make everything turn out good.

Most people just don't want to think about life as a pizza.

Broken Wings

There is an amazing tiny book by a Paul Gallico, The Snow Goose, 1940, that haunts me to this very day.

WWII Dunkirk

To me there is only one recorded version to listen to which is with Herbert Marshal… in the 50's. If I played it now I would still cry. (see footnote at bottom)

Whether it is a bird or a pet or anything innocent, if it is broken we are drawn to help it. When the Snow Goose flew again… so did I. Just an old vinyl record….

In life, we cannot avoid seeing broken wings. Every person we meet has something that needs to heal. So that flight they never imagined could take place. There are the obvious addicted and withdrawn eyes that confirm a brokenness. Afraid to be helped. Then there are the seemingly normal people who have their busy lives, though deep down inside they wish some private thoughts were better. Often accepting dreams as impossible dreams.

"In life, we cannot avoid seeing broken wings."

If you can see a brokenness you think about ways you may help before moving on. For a broken wing requires holding and attention and time.

As one's heart plays a more and more important role in one's life one can feel more of the hurt out there. The numbers can be frightening. Yet those you can easily help is now obvious... Spirit is uplifted as one makes a difference.

To be close to someone when they fly again is humbling and breathtaking.

It is why we are here.

Godspeed my Snow Goose.

On to Dunkirk.

Footnote: Listen To *The Snow Goose* on Youtube https://youtu.be/eo-1bK7h5iA

Good Hair

Good hair seems more important than good health.

Why do all the TV weather announcers have good hair?

From all the magazines it seems like every woman has shiny hair with soft curls.

You go in the grocery store and you see a lot of bad hair.

Now color can be amazing. Am sure we all have our secret preferences...

Hair care is more important than child care? Bet all the hair product sold could pay for all the nation's health care needs.

Now everybody does not have good hair. Some are very self-conscious if their hair is too curly or too straight or too whatever. Always comparing one's own with others. Always.

Color, highlights, roots, split ends... and it never stops.

What is wrong with me? It must be my hair... LOL

Now we should look more closely at those who have bad hair. Do they seem unhappy? What about those of us with little hair… you know the old bald eagles… Then why are there so many bad, weird haircuts on guys? The NBA has some really bad hair making baskets. I bet they are going to choke at pictures of themselves 20 years from now!

Hair used to be a little more uniform. Now it screams diversity…… or chaos????

Hair is long, hair is short, heads are shaved, heads are never shaved. Dreadlocks on guys who do not look hip….. bad.

I wonder what kind of hair you get to have in heaven?

Heavenly curls?

Michelle and Cecile cut my hair.

Who cuts yours?

Inside they are good people.

Crowd Size

My crowd is bigger than your crowd.

My dad is bigger than your dad.

My big brother is going to get you.

So who cares??

Unless you get beat up.

Have you been a President standing in front of a million people giving an inaugural address?? Get a life. Show some respect. The Donald thinks big and has big plans. It is about time... Hello?? I bet we all will be singing a different tune in a year or two.

We need a big military. We are a good people and must be respected for that. There is good and there is Evil. We no longer have time to deliberate and intellectualize about perfect world concepts. They don't work.

For us to protect the world we have to be strong. Stronger than hell. It is time to look inward and address drug abuse

"My crowd is bigger than your crowd."

for what it is … EVIL. It is destroying our youth and culture. We look up to false images and celebrity as if they were the answer.

The answer lies within if we weren't so lazy. We pander to feelings. We are lost in the crowd size applauding us.

The Donald has rewritten the book on crowd size. His rallies across the nation were unimaginable. Crowd sizes that dumfounded the experts. Media downplayed their size and enthusiasm. It should have been exciting and positive to the pundits. Talk, talk, talk. A lexicon of repetition and trying to sound important... Vanity? Since when is a reporter the final judge?

Crowd size means nothing in front of a machine gun.

It is the heart and the will of the crowd that wins the battle.

Do not count the Donald out…….

Super Bowl

Lady GaGa will not do the Super Bowl Coin Toss.

She is being forced to sing.

Fortunately George H. W. Bush has agreed to fill in and bring some class to the moment.

This football game is for the championship of all sports hearts. We raise our kids in sports. Participating in sports allows a mom and dad and son and daughter to enjoy victory and defeat. From sandlot baseball in Iowa to tarmac in Brooklyn we spend endless hours in team camaraderie. It is pure. Cheating does not work. Disrespect for the rules means you get kicked out… and not to sensitivity training…

Sports brings families together. Sports bring the nation together for one moment. The flag is raised and praised. Hands over hearts or in salute as we sing the National Anthem. Politics does not belong here. It is our sports church.

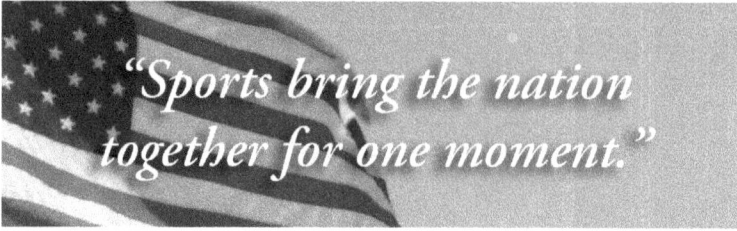

"Sports bring the nation together for one moment."

Opposing teams and fans have fun in the intensity of the rivalries. But it is good fun. You can hug your buddy afterwards even though he won and you lost. Yearlong trash talk lightens up every barbeque.

Being a celebrity is an enormous burden as privacy is stripped away. Being vain and insecure is part of the deal. The challenge to greatness is found in humility. Is found in being champions of the Truth... and I do mean in the Biblical sense. That is class.

I hope for Lady GaGa to make a decision that will ennoble her. That will unite rather than divide. What a shame to waste all this talent in the desecration of the great event she was honored to be invited to. Pray for her.

The Super Bowl can only remain super if we don't self-destruct half-time on the 50 yard line.

President Bush, could you help us again?

Bonnie Gossip

Bonnie gossip is Scottish. Lassie's talking about kilts…
LOL

Gossip keeps lips active all over the world. It doesn't have to be true, it just has to be new.

Wives can't wait to go to the grocery store because as they check out they can scan all the gossip magazine covers. Mostly about unhappy celebrities in some kind of self-induced jam. One wonders how one would feel if we were in their shoes?

Gossip seldom does good. It too often never stays the same and can't be trusted. Except that we want to trust it.… Crazy?

Wouldn't it be great if only good gossip would be printed… or at least 50% good… so gossip could have redeeming value? Maybe government could help and create the NGA, a National Gossip Agency. Where items could be investigated and assigned Truth indexes…??

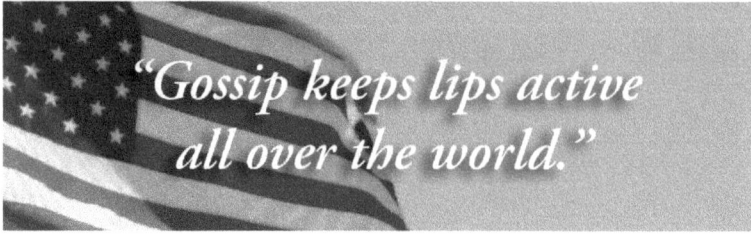

Did you ever wonder if clergy gossiped? Bet they have to hear a lot.

I bet if one added up one's weekly gossip minutes and then gave a dollar for each minute to a charity... gossip could make a big difference in all lives. Just sayin'.

Now Bonnie is a Scotch word. Wonder how much gossip goes on in Scotland? Over drinking scotch?? Lips loosen and things are whispered in fleeting sincerity.

Wonder if the French and Swiss gossip as much?

Are you allowed to gossip in the Middle-East?

Bet no one gossips north of the 38th parallel.

"Bonnie is hot".

Now that's gossip...

Just In Time

It is never too late.

When all hope is gone.

The "never expected" happens.

Just in time.

There is a lot of bad in the world.

Everyone needs to be rescued at least once in their life. Special heroes are required to be lowered from helicopters to hoist you up from the flames or the sinking boat. They are often called angels. But I thought angels came from some other place way in the heavens??

Our mothers exist to protect us when we are most vulnerable. Which, for some, could be as long as they are alive…

Our nation needs protection from the Evil within and without. War seems just a breath away. Who do we send just in time?

> ## "Everyone needs to be rescued at least once in their life."

Maybe the kind word you give to a stranger will be just in time…. And you will never know it.

Maybe the first "I'm proud of you" a person has ever heard?

It is never too late to help someone else. Look more carefully around you every day. Attack the frown. Attack the sadness. Attack the superficial. There is always something to attack just in time.

Most people are in denial about their self-worth. Not feeling they are good enough.

Many escape to the good feelings of drugs and addiction. And drain their souls of purpose.

Not unlike all our frivolous diversions… from cell phone to television…swallowing enormous portions of our day. A twisted addiction that allows one to avoid reality and responsibility.

A place is needed for all to go. To reform. To be dignified.

For some it could be the military.

For some it may be a church.

There is this "Just-in-time" Place in Naples Florida.......
hmmm...

Tis of Thee

My country… is facing challenges greater than ever. Who would have believed…?

Elections were chaos… media lost leadership. Nobody knows what to believe any more. So we turn away. Never from our flag. Patriotism is going underground. The flag has been singled out as a symbol of distorted conservative religious propaganda. The left cries foul.

Red, white, and blue is still waving in the mind. Only veterans and police now salute her. All schools used to. No more. Betsy Ross has shed a tear.

There has to be a symbol of what we stand for other than a nuclear submarine. The flag will remain that. Too many have given their blood defending her. We must stand up to the forces of denial and salute again. All of us.

Our congress works for us. They act like spoiled brats never agreeing. It is time for all their sons to go into the military. It is time for them to worry for their lives and their flag.

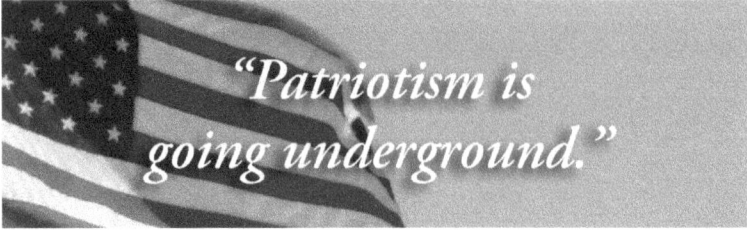

Our nation deserves better. Our House and Senate should be fine-tuned like special operations commands. Trained to get the job done without months of dithering. They are so inefficient that it is a disgrace. Maybe they should all sit mixed up so they can't avoid each other.

They use the same bathrooms??? Or is some toilet paper printed with donkeys or elephants?

How about term limits? The government is of thee. It should be run like a business… with benefits under control.

Pray it doesn't take a war with someone to bring us together.

"Long may our land be bright,

With freedom's holy light

Protect us by thy might,

Great God our King."

Stone Age

My friend is a stone mason.

He carries large rocks and hand chisels them into wall pieces. Handmade foundations of sweat and probably a little cursing. Then he goes to church. LOL

His life is physical. Unlike most professions... mind and extra body goes into every long hour of the day. The result lasts forever. Stone foundations.

What our country is lacking is the understanding that for something to be good it takes real effort not entitlement. Most of our immigrant population are honored to have hard work that pays... for where they come from it does not. Let's stop slamming our country and rebuild her. From infrastructure to bureaucracy we need to reorganize and refocus.

Our forefathers laid a great foundation for us to build on, not to dilute with lawsuits.

Why can't our schools teach foundational values? Why?

"My friend is a stone mason."

Why is a teacher not free to teach? To teach from the heart? Stone by stone?

Right now we have indulged ourselves on a path back to the Stone Age. To empty quarries in the mind.

Unless we look in the mirror with honesty we will see no reflection. Other than the reflection of lost hopes and dreams. A wasteland for generations to come. Or maybe where large bureaucratic dinosaurs consume our every breath. Or maybe extinction.

The percentage of the human race being stoned continues to rise.

Is this the harbinger of our new stoned age???

Mother Power

The womb was room enough. Cozy, warm, assuring.

Then…. No more pain for mom…. Or… has it just begun?

Mother is the power that fills the young inquiring eyes with Truth. Her affirmation is always there. We feel her pride.

Life does all it can to dismember the family. Parents must be assertive to protect their growing child. You always listen even when you pretend you are not. You care that she cares. She is your power. You are hers. Both should be proud that each is proud. This is important.

The power of the womb should be respected by all. Conceived in love, born in love, and lived in love…..

Mothers served us.

All world leaders must serve us better. With humility and appreciation. Isn't that what they are supposed to do? Is not a President a servant? Is not a politician a servant? Is not a doctor a servant? Is not a CEO a servant? In fact, aren't we all meant to serve if we are to mean something?

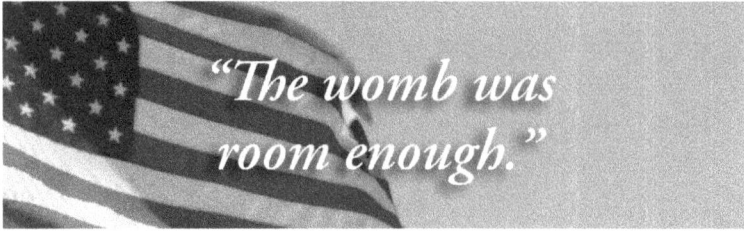

"The womb was room enough."

What about worldwide child and women's abuse? Is not the United Nations our worldwide servant? Should they not listen to and protect all mothers?

Mothers have the power to demand that the umbilical cords be cut between waste and hypocrisy and abuse. In government and in bureaucracy and in all societies.

All have mothers.

All should be on their knees saying...

Mom, what should I do?"

Law Full

Every law now has a new law which will soon get a subset law that will be codified or whatever.

Laws about laws are now filling the airwaves and internet with attractive promises of payoffs if you meet the detailed criteria of qualification… Ha! I am sounding like them. They promise to protect and make fairness reign. Except that fairness must result in payments and payoffs.

Who else can we turn to for fairness and justice? The police are constrained by process. Common sense may be uncommon now as fear of legislation looms.

In battle, there is no time for courts. Shoot or be shot.

There is something funny going on here. We all know what good and bad is. Or we think we do. Except that both have been broken up into a million opinions. The truth no longer is clear. "Take or be took."

"In battle, there is no time for courts."

If we don't believe in God then we become godless, and are appointing ourselves as the final arbiters of good and Evil... of sane and insane. Think about the consequences.

We are so full of law that we are its new slaves.

If you want to think independently you may now be breaking the law. Pretty soon a lawyer will be riding in every squad car. To read you your rights before the officer is allowed to fire.

I know this is all silly.

Does your heart still have a chance?

It knows what is right and wrong.

Wonder where that comes from?

Sue me.

Love Act

Is it an act?

The worst crime in the world is to play with love.

Love defines truth. We cannot survive without both.

The first time you feel that feeling you know it is important. You can't take your mind off it.

It keeps a man and a woman joined even when 5,000 miles apart. The military knows it for sure. Letters from home are clutched tightly to the heart. Top left pocket.

One has no problem taking any bullet to protect family.

To protect a child.

To protect love.

To protect the flag.

Why?

Why is it worth it? That is a love act. To give up your life for another. To give up your life for all....

"The worst crime in the world is to play with love."

Fools for love? If not for Love then for what?

With Love in your heart you see and feel the need of others. You can't turn away if love has its say. Be it a kind gesture, an arm around a shoulder, or a verbal pat on the back… love can be sent by you to make the small difference. Maybe planting a seed and positive memory for the one your heart chose.

A servant heart is one on the hunt for sadness and insecurity. To reassure and reaffirm.

The act of serving can rebuild a family, community, business, and nation.

This is no act.

This is Love.

A Buddy Died

They pounded their Tridents onto the coffin.

Salutes.

A new flag in Arlington.

A folded one handed to a wife.

A mother's hand on her shoulder.

Kids dressed up.

Buddies at attention.

Fingers pulling triggers, jarring the stillness.

Buddies are important.

They offer their lives as protection.

I swam with some.

One was my Golden Retriever.

"A new flag in Arlington."

His name was "Buddy".

We lost him last night.

This is Love.

Never Forgive

It feels good to say "I will never forgive you". Never Forgive. It is a threat and an empowering statement. Don't mess with me.

But it is also too late if the act to be forgiven has already done its harm. "You slandered my family!" "You desecrated my flag." "You mocked my God." "I will never forgive." "You stole my money." "You wrecked my car." "You killed my dog." "You are history." "I am coming for you in the night."

Red lines must be red lines. Someone must draw them. Otherwise there is nothing to fear if you are Evil. Punishment must be more than words. Sometimes it must be violent and massively deadly. Innocent bystanders getting consumed in the flames. Their families will never forgive.

Deep inside no one escapes guilt. Insecurity is rampant and demands more Evil and selfishness to stay ahead of the pain. But deep down they know.

"Red lines must be red lines."

Defiance must come before compassion. The only way out is Faith or death… possibly eternal…

Hate will be borne until one realizes that it is a private cancer robbing one of potential. To become who you were meant to be means you have to be free of negative burdens. You must find a way to forgive so you can move on.

Tragedy and intentional tragedy are bridges down on your highway. Forgiveness is the only bridge. To never forgive is to never know what is waiting on the other side.

Is forgiveness possible?

That is everyone's private journey.

You are at a Cross-Road.

Due North

I can remember the phrase "Due North" since way back as a kid.

First compass?

North Star?

You got all your bearings from due North. Had to know it was right to plot courses. Whether sextants at sea or compass at land True North had to be known.

If you just kept heading due north you will reach one spot, no matter where in the world you are…. The North Pole… You may even see Santa or the Truth. True North….. Get it?

If you go due west or due east, due left or due right… you will be going around in giant circles.

You gotta know where you are going!! Or you will end up nowhere and probably at the bottom of some ocean. This

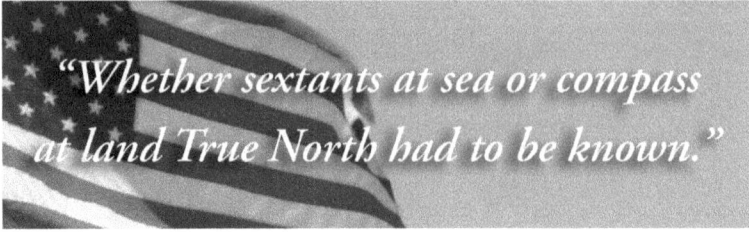

goes for the psychological. You will go crazy if you don't get to the right place. The place where you really belong.

Your compass becomes the person next to you... With the darting, insecure eyes.... Hungry for a helping hand or pat on the back. That is true north. Go in that direction.

Helping others in the smallest of ways will put you on an alarming journey and you will become somebody. You will find true pride within. And new smiles for all to see. You will never look back.

Your compass is in your heart.

You become a compass.

You become a True North for others.

Future Shredder

I shred a lot of invoices.

It's a cross cut shredder.

Impossible to reconstruct and glean any confidential information.

Once you are in the shredder you don't exist. You can't say what you are or were.... I shredded a résumé this morning. Nice gal, educated, interesting background.... On paper.... But she only wanted to work a few days a week and not on weekends and only for a month.

Something terrifying is going on. Social networks? Schools? Parents? High expectations with minimal effort. Social skills diminished. More and more of the young and unemployed feel entitled. Why can't they be the carefree person in a company with generous benefits, breaks, vacations...and a 5-day work week?? It is "What can the company do for me?"

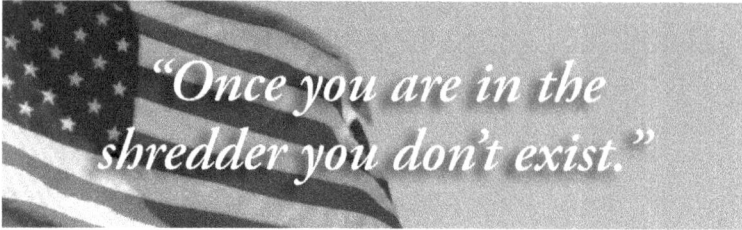

This is cultural suicide. Help-Wanted signs are everywhere. Résumés are left at offices only to create eligibility for unemployment. Eligible for what? Drugs?

That noise in the distance...?? Shredders working overtime.

A young gal from Cuba is grateful to have any employment. Back home there was none. She excels in every way. Manners, poise, and dedication is insuring her a future. Attitude and effort exemplary.

Hard to find excellence locally.

What is being taught in our schools?? Are ethics, honesty, responsibility, initiative, respect, hard work, and reality no longer taught? No longer the underpinnings of a conversation. What has been taken from the teacher?

Maybe there will soon be cost cutting. Teacher robots without emotion will teach. Virtual reality glasses on all. Except that reality is being detached from reality.

The future shredder is here.

Shredding our futures.

Starving dreams.

Denying dignity.

Enabling Evil.

Pray for us.

Cross Pen

A Cross pen was a status symbol.

Silver or gold, filled or solid.

They stood out in your shirt in the old days. The only problem lay in their beauty. They were too thin to hold and press on for a long time.

They made nice gifts. But, as in life, it is not about the pen, but the writer. It is not about the tool, but rather what is done with it. What do we bring to the table? A 14KT ball point pen does not make the writer elegant. It is only the words in ink that matter. And where those words come from. And where those words go.

Someone said a long time ago… "Sticks and stones can break your bones but words can never hurt you"… This worked until it didn't. With the sensitivity overindulgence these days… you can be on the evening news if you say anything politically *incorrect*.

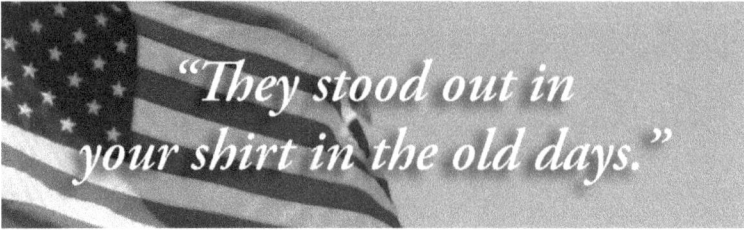

Words can be speeches. Assembled by word specialists. Image manipulators breathing fake passion into the overthought work of appeasement. Cheers and clapping at camouflaged boredom. Pats on the back all around during the cocktail reception. LOL.

Words can accomplish a lot. Take the Declaration of Independence. Lawyers are still trying to unwind it. They can't. Because it was from the hearts of a few.

The only writer worth reading is one who uses his heart as the pen.

Any of us can write if it comes from the heart.

And you don't have to use blood as the ink.

Drone Dragon

Dragons are only seen in scary movies.

Flying serpents.

They breathe fire and stand up roaring.

They frighten kids only.

Though they may still be seen in the skies of Tibet...

Coming down and ruining picnics.... LOL

Predators are large dragon-like flying drones.

They capture all the information from above and send fire and missiles down to reap destruction. Hopefully never missing their Evil targets.

Today there is a new noise up in the skies. A high-pitched faint buzzing. You can't see them but they are videoing all that they see. Some take pretty pictures of fancy homes to be sold. Houses come alive with intrigue as they are filmed at sunset from above. Magical marketing.

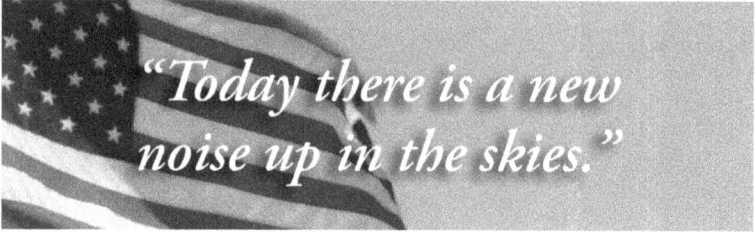

"Today there is a new noise up in the skies."

The police use them to track Evil people unseen. When just high enough you will not hear the buzz of the blades. You can buy your drone from Amazon Prime and have it in two days from $100 to… I even saw one for $32,000.….!! Then you can spy on your neighbor or explore the beauty of nature…. Or make films for those who never get to see much….

You see…drones can now be dragons bringing truth to hopeful eyes. Faith can be restored with honest interpretations of reality.

Go buy one and make your world better.

Plus they are more fun than a motorcycle!

Go buzz Bentley's………

Permit-Able

"Mother May I?" is an old children's game.

I think it was a ruse to teach the concepts of permission and manners and respect for authority.

Hey, maybe it should be a new TV show for adults?? Or... How about "Donkeys May I?" or "Elephants May I?"... Get it?? What has happened to manners??? Everything that use to be respected is now disrespected.

This has created a regulatory bonanza for the government. We are asking slow, tedious, over compensated bureaucracy bureaucrats to manage permissions of all sorts. These are called "Permits". They permit you to do whatever. There may be more permits than our population!!

Technology is outpacing bureaucracy's ability to devise new permits to protect us. Our insatiable need for regulatory decisions is fueling the legal profession and law enforcement agencies. Anything that can have a permit will. Are you permit-able?

"This has created a regulatory bonanza for the government."

Before we became so intelligent there was common sense. Unwritten laws that the law-abiding would honor and you moved along more efficiently. Something was driving honesty and goodness. Values from the old-country? Europe... steeped in moral underpinnings yet tainted by horrific injustice and abuse.

Today every nation has its laws. Many are just insane. Allowing inhuman interpretations. Permits have not solved our problem

We are the problem. Until each finds his heart and purpose, respect will continue to diminish. Evil is having a field day as the next permit crawls its way through the bureaucracy before being applauded by the media... And is outdated.

Is there a permit to allow you to help others?

Don't ask.

Just do it.

Remote Inn

Way up in the mountains.

Maybe a high altitude valley with a stream, meadows, trees up the mountainside…maybe Switzerland, maybe… a log cabin with porch and 3 bedrooms and 3 baths, large screen TV and open floor plan….and garage for Land Rover…and even Wifi.

Remote is changing quickly these days. It is where you get away to and just take in what is real and quiet. So quiet that you may hear a deer's footstep….. That you may hear the heartbeat reflected in the mirror. You may hear it smiling… and saying …"follow me".

This is the Remote Inn. Trip Advisor 5 star rated. One caveat. No directions currently available on GPS.

How do we get there? Is there a gas station on the way or do we have to load up with 5 gallon cans? Food? Can our two kids and golden retriever "Buddy" make it? We have got to get there. Together. We have to find the Remote Inn so

> "There are all kinds of places of peace."

we can be a family together in the beauty of the infinity of nature. Please dear God....

There are all kinds of places of peace. None are easy to get to. People tell you about them but there are no maps. So, if you want to go, you have to trust your instincts. Keeping doubt stored in the back behind the spare tire.

"We are on our way!" fills the car.

"Thanks Dad".

When I am away I remote in to my Bible Study in Maine.

New Life Form

It was a new life form from a rock in Mars... It invaded the space station. Horrific stuff. I stopped the movie halfway through. We have enough new life forms already to try to contain.

Heck, look at the atrocity of the Middle-East. Terrifying things happen every day to innocent people and children. No movie. And more horrific than any special effects can create. The soldier comes back from wherever there is hell and clams up. No one should see what he has. He withdraws to find direction and purpose. He has done his bit.... what about us??

We have allowed ourselves to be so beaten down by the sensitivities of others that we don't know what we stand for. Those who do are silent. The silent majority accepting the drip torture of inaction.

Step back. Find a mirror. Anywhere. Now. In the gas station.....

"*I stopped the movie halfway through.*"

Maybe the new life form should be me? One is always concerned with the outside, while the inside drifts….. The oceans inside are often left unsailed….

When you dive beneath a surface you can find a new quiet and new eyes. Any surface.

It takes courage to take that breath, pivot, and descend into the depths at night. Maybe if you turn and ascend, following your bubbles, the light of a new moon will free you. Maybe you can be a new life form to yourself. A life form that searches for injustice to right, for hunger to feed, for the hurt to console, for anyone to serve.

That is our calling.

That is why we hide so much inside.

All are desperate to be a new life form.

Smart Balance

It says 20 calories less than butter; O mg of cholesterol versus 30 mg for butter. How in the world did civilization make it so far without Smart Balance? I like the olive oil version. Gets me closer to Italy.

America is overweight. Americans consume salt, sugar, and fast foods faster than anyone. We are #1. We like easy answers and gossip centric news. Celebrity lives are held up as exemplary. Dreams are fulfilled on TV.... Soon to be replaced by virtual reality accessories. Self-indulgent wandering youth protest causes with no commitment. International injustice and Evil are ignored as if fiction. There is no balance.

Government is supposed to provide a framework for freedom and balance. Governments struggle with sustaining themselves. Separate planets. Physical borders are trespassed. Moral boundaries are mocked. Dishonesty is now a tool. Leadership is no longer from within.

Parents are giving in. Schools are giving up. Government is giving nothing but everything. Spoiled is the new entitlement. The cell phone is the new mirror. You see what you want to see, except it is exactly what you don't want to see. Social network is really a net that works on addicting you. Our life is under attack by pop up ads. Just wait the 15 seconds to see a managed truth. Why bother? Do "likes" really matter???

I want to pull off the plastic lid and get the real Smart Balance.

I think that lid is really a black leather cover....

Reach Out

I am reaching out to the few remaining of us who still speak "cool". English is no longer a course in schools. So, there are no more rules. Grammar becomes an elitist concept.

"Reaching out" is giving me muscle cramps in my arms. Maybe if I extended them holding 10 pound weights I will be stronger to reach out to more.....???

They are no longer saying "cool". It is now "sweet".

"No worries" means "forget it". Don't worry as that assessment has already been made for you.

"Sounds good" drives me nuts. You mean what is good only sounds so? Meaning it is really not a commitment? Not a firm endorsement that it is good and that you fully endorse it? Does "good" have a sound?

Something is going on. This guy had a full tattoo on the lower half of his face and couldn't figure out why he couldn't get a job..... "No worries"... "sweet".....".sounds good"....".whatever"

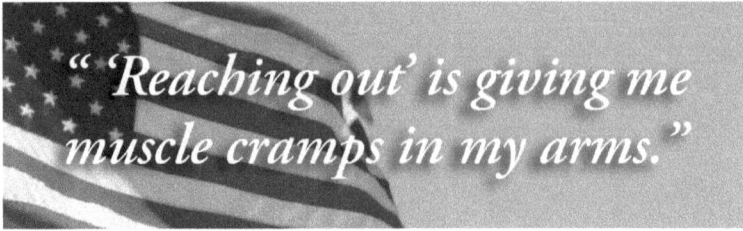

" 'Reaching out' is giving me muscle cramps in my arms."

Maybe our individuality is becoming our god. You can always find 100 people on Facebook that will "like" you no matter how imperfect you are…LOL. Evil people can find 100 people if not thousands who think they "sound good" and flip them a "like". So…. they feel good about themselves.

"Advice" is no longer acceptable as it hurts feelings. Advice is inflammatory. Only social network affirmation is valid.

No shaking of hands. The non-committal fist bump takes less than a second.

I know this sounds cynical…but every departing generation has earned its right to proclaim "enough!".

I am reaching out to the wisdom buried in your hearts.

Sound good??

Whatever……

Fake Truth

Thousands of years ago how did anyone know what was the Truth?

It was all like that game where you get a line of people, (it's really fun with kids as a teaching tool) and whisper something in the first person's ear. Like "It is important to respect your mother"… and everyone whispers it to the person next to them. By the time it gets to the end you ask the last person to say what she was told…it comes out…. "My mother yells at me"….

Ok that is what the journey of the Truth was like from Nazareth to Rome….. or today from Paris to New York… Or from your best friend to you. Something happens along the way. Look at the debate going on today in the media. Who is to know what the Truth is. Solution, Turn it off. What is not the Truth is becoming more important than what is.

"*Who is to know what the Truth is?*"

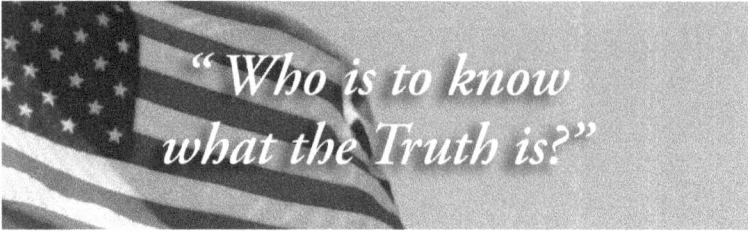

There is Evil afoot… We need Special Operations Truth Snipers to do their powerful words unseen. Where are the leaders of Truth? Everyone claims to be.

It's unverifiable chaos.

Who can you Trust?

Is there a smart phone that can call the Lord?

Would we believe Him now??

I don't think we have a choice.

And dat's da Twooth!

The Blacksmith

What does forge mean?

Valley Forge???

"Forge ahead men."… Sounds like a WW1 command in some God-awful trench. Forge ahead to an unlikely victory… and more likely to a gruesome death in some mud in Europe.

Something that is made in a forge is made in great heat with enormous power, pounding, and finesse. Horseshoes to swords. Art to car frames. Molten metals poured, cooled, and shaped. And sharpened into something that lasts.

What about values??

How are they forged?

How do you get both children and men forged into strength, honesty, and humility?

Many more men today do not choose a journey that will make them strong. Social networks often prop up weakness.

"The hard Way is the easy Way."

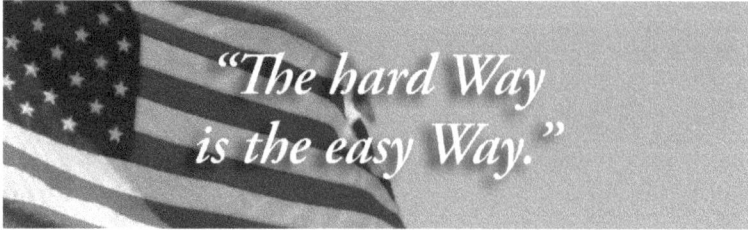

No one wants to be yelled at by a Drill Instructor, much less by any authority…even father or mother…… or wife….???

There has to be a better way? Except there isn't.

Hard work, repetitive work, sweat, and pain yield wisdom and certitude. There is no easy way. The hard Way is the easy Way.

Honesty forges trust.

Compassion forges humility.

Freedom forges creativity.

Love forges hope.

The womb forges a breath.

That puts first mist on the mirror.

What do you want to be?

T-Bone

We all have favorite places to get a good steak.

I am still looking for it…. Great that is….

And we all have favorite cuts and memories.

A week ago I was introduced to a new cut… my T-bone. I was in NH picking up a new black lab puppy and while driving home I met the T-bone. A bright flash of white is all I remember. Was it heaven? My buddy was driving and the concrete block truck hit us broadside. God knows what speed he was travelling at. We both climbed out dazed. Nothing broken. A lot of pain for me for a week, then… it went away. My wife and a lot of prayers must have played a role.

So I am alive to write again today.

Feeling blessed to be alive, I am free of everyone who may criticize. They don't matter. "Free at last, free at last…"

Part of how our nation reached this current frightening divisiveness is because we have become prisoners of our own

"So I am alive to write today."

take on history and truth. Minds made up. History screwed up. Futures screwed up. Families screwed up. Government screwed up.

Too much not going right. Evil scurrying around everywhere. Evil masquerading as truth.

I am not the only one who has been T-boned.

We all have.

By trucks loaded with blocks of ignorance.

Tweet

Tweets can be sweet, but for the most part they aren't.

Tweet on Twitter and reveal how intelligent you are, much less how funny…

Instant mockery at one's fingertips.

This is the new norm… to be able to comment on anyone and anything at any time to please one's self. And… since the normal tendency is to continue to please oneself you are limited to 140 characters. This is actually a phenomenal gift as it becomes grammar school for most. To actually say something in only 140 characters or like 20 words…. Makes up for all the "sensitivity" sensitivity in English classes…. If those classes still exist… LOL.

We have the President to thank for making tweets part of our new culture… Freedom of expression can be constructive and it is certainly nice to know *what* he and others are thinking. Step back… there are some important issues here…..

*"There is no sanitizer
for fake tweets yet."*

Tweets are also magnifying our cultural divisions and bringing them to the light. Yet there is so much information and opinion now that knowledge is being turned into porridge. Vacations are now downloading opportunities in once peaceful settings. Go to the beach and look at the faces getting no sun as they are looking down... LOL

We are being tweeted to death.

Individuality is becoming consensus driven.

There is no sanitizer for fake tweets yet.

Scuba diving looks like one of the few retreats.....

As long as your air lasts...

Hate Group

I hate sweet potatoes.

My wife loves them.

I hate pain.

Avoiding it is a ballet.

I finally hate half-truths.

They are lies.

I hate selfishness and arrogance. I can see it so much more clearly in my old age.

Some things in life that one hates can be avoided. Getting near hate is very dangerous. Anything can happen… and will… We have government and religion to protect us from hate.

Government does it with laptops, churches with pews. That is old news.

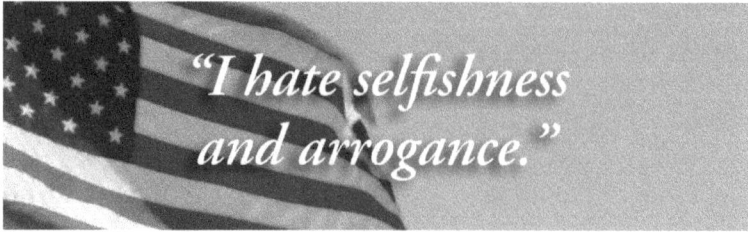

"*I hate selfishness and arrogance.*"

When we were young, we all wanted to be a member of a group... to have an identity. Group, club, fraternity, boy scouts, gang. Groups protect their members.

When one grows up you find out that you are very unique, and are uncomfortable with groups which tend to take away one's individuality and freedom of thinking... group think is risky too. I never formed a "We Hate Sweet Potatoes" group. Could have turned violent...??? Could have lost lots of friends over it.

In today's upside-down world hate groups are rapidly multiplying. This is not good. Is it?

We should be hating evil, except what is good is now being twisted into evil.

The flag, the Cross???

A church/prayer center is being petitioned to remove the Cross on her steeple...which has been there a long time... and in the minds of man for 2,000 years. Go figure?

We should be celebrating our heritage, our foundational values, our history, our military, our law-enforcement, our church diversity, and our hearts.

We are no longer teaching what is good.

We are allowing the haters to accuse us of hate.

I hate the silence of Christians.

Blame Game

"I did it" is no longer an indicator of manhood.

Can anyone remember the days when one felt compelled to tell your mother the truth?? "Mom, I did it." When telling the truth was more important than anything else?

What about the "Pledge of Allegiance"?

"Do you solemnly swear….?"

Trust is dead, long live blame.

When someone does something right he is blamed for not doing it sooner. Interviews are discarded until one fits the blame story. Is the reporter to blame? Are we to blame?

When someone is murdered there is always somebody to blame and the courts to confirm it. Jurors debate and assign the blame.

But who are the jurors of false or distorted blame?? How do the silent chime in? How are their church bells heard?

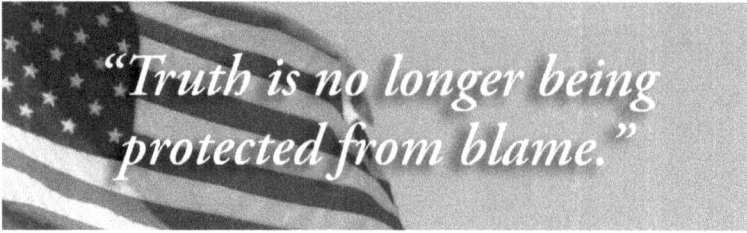

Truth is no longer being protected from blame. Is this a game??

Crazy, upside-down, reasoning based on opinion not truth. Since when is opinion so powerful? Since when is blame the only arbiter of truth? How are decent people to sort out all this mess? Minds are being meddled with by blamers. I wish the media could be turned to in the fight against excessive blaming.

Funny, I tried watching the news last night with my solar eclipse glasses and saw a lot of long Pinocchio noses.

Hey, who is to blame??

Ninety-Nine

"Ninety-nine bottles of beer on the wall, ninety-nine bottles of beer...."

Those were the years and those were the road trips. In celebration of being young, alive, and dumb. Now not dumb disrespectfully, but dumb to all that there was to learn in the future.

Youth is a symphony of searching and fun unless life has dealt you the card of instant maturing with a broken family or poverty or bad luck.

Then all the smiles in the world on TV can't put the past back together again.

Bottles begin to fall as the years go by. You could live until 99, but a lot has to fall in place to reach it.

Decisions about right and wrong had better be right. There is no going back to this liquor store....

Alcohol is also extremely dangerous because it comes with so many seductive smiles. I know families that do not drink

"There is no going back to this liquor store..."

at all... and these are off the charts special. It doesn't seem possible. But it is. Think of all the time wasted when one could have been helping someone else.

Crazy? I am not so sure.

Deep down inside all riddles can be answered.

This book is full of them.

Especially the 99th bottle.

Godspeed y'all.

Bottoms up.

Toll Booth

Don't pay. Don't play.

It's that simple. We all want to get on the highway as we know where we are going. We will get there more quickly, barring an accident or stupidly running out of gas.

In life you have to pay to play. Drinks cost. Dinners cost. Families cost. Cars cost. Hobbies cost. Schools cost. Travels cost. Doctors cost. Protection costs.

What doesn't cost? Is life just one big toll booth? A hand or robot reaching out for your cash?

Everything we do wrong takes its toll.

You can pay tolls in advance or on your credit card automatically. But you are paying one way or another. There are no free passes in life.

The more "good" one does the fewer the tolls. In fact, helping others will usually bring a bigger return that will make any tolls seem minimal. Think about it. The more

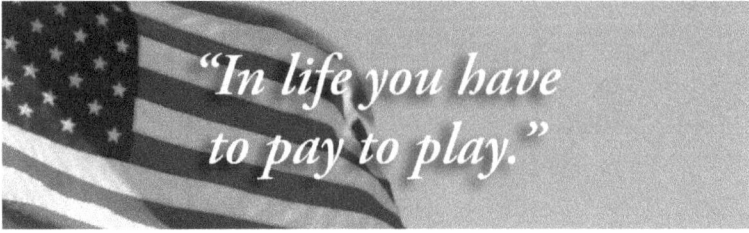

"In life you have to pay to play."

good one does unselfishly the less the pain and the less the payment. In fact you get credits on your account!

You can beat the toll booth after all! You can now drive through the tolls smiling.

Oh, I forgot to mention that I say "God Bless You" to the toll collector.

Surprisingly they respond in kind…. Toll free driving…..

Helicopter

There it was, 50 years ago in the middle of the night, alone in the south Atlantic. I signaled it to pick me up. Training makes it second nature.

Ships start to sink and the helicopter finds the lucky clinging on.

What does an angel look like? Go to Rome and you will see every kind on the ceilings... suspended.... From a helicopter?

What is an angel? Maybe it is anyone who helps someone else? Maybe you are one to the person helped. If you do it quietly and move on, then you must be an angel...?

Texas got to see some helicopter angels this week. But then is not the guy in the small outboard going down the flooded street to a house with a family reaching him in waist deep water a helicopter??? An angel? There is no damned politics waist deep in neighborhood waters.

"What does an angel look like?"

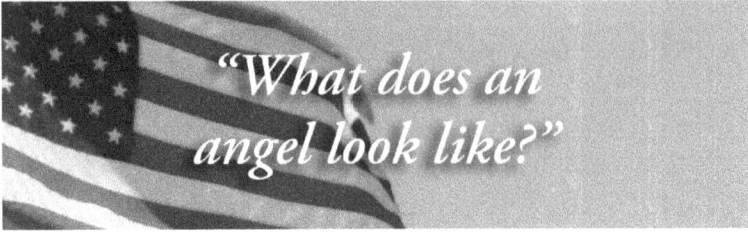

This is a great opportunity for the media and politicians to put clothes pins on their lips and smile through their pain at the good that is being done regardless of opinion. Democrats and Republicans wading together waist deep in water... for a "first"... (Get it?)

We are a nation unlike any other in its ability to treat pain and injustice locally...

Helicopters are great for extraction. Looking up into their sun one can only see an angel.

Wouldn't it be fun to fly a helicopter?

Just find someone in need and damn the politics.

Hope

I hope it gets better.

I hope I won't get aborted.

I hope daddy won't leave mommy.

I hope that soldiers will not have to die.

I hope that I will still get hugs.

I hope that bad people can't say they are good.

I hope that they raise the flag again at school.

I hope that TV goes back to being black and white.

I hope that electric cars don't kill the roar of exhausts.

I hope that they take the commercials off the weather channels.

I hope that politicians sit and eat mixed in with each other.

I hope that polls are no longer necessary.

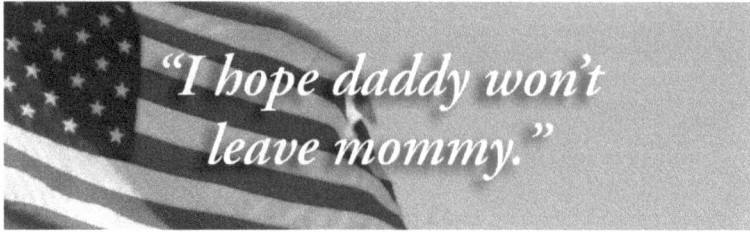

"*I hope daddy won't leave mommy.*"

I hope that someday a person will answer the phone.

I hope that everyone can come for Thanksgiving.

I hope that my Christmas tree still has a Nativity scene.

Is that too much to hope?

Your Story

What floor are you on in that high rise?

Higher floors are more expensive.

Some cost fortunes… Wonder if it's because they are closer to heaven?? Status? Helps tell who you are?? They know you are rich because of your story.

Everyone is born on the same floor. It is the Womb.

From there all hell breaks loose. Unless you are lucky.

Parents argue, parents leave. Seeds of doubt and insecurity are planted. That drives many to fight for wealth to protect them. To hide the hurt.

The lucky feel love and truth and grow strong. Strong, not spoiled.

Today the social networks are creating false support and false love. It is hard to know the truth. It is hard to know how you can be a meaningful person.

> *"The lucky feel love and truth and grow strong."*

It takes decades for "Your Story" to reach its final chapters.
To see who you became or who you were meant to be.
Many chapters seemed painful. Mistakes made. People hurt.

But how did your story end up?

Did you get there?

And where?

Did you eventually like your story?

Or was the last chapter not worth reading?

Why Me

Is this not a universal expression?

We had one in the Teams.... "S..t happens"

To everyone.

Why is my nose too big? Why am I not rich? My mother needs full time care. Why me?

We criticize ourselves and our luck most of our life. We regret our "flaws" and our "mistakes". There is so much most don't like about themselves. Why did things have to turn out so rough? Why doesn't everybody like me?

If one does not step back from their mirror, they will never see the beautiful potential of their uniqueness. Every scar, every injury, every hurt, every love propels one to potentials not ever imagined. "Yeah, sure... go away...."

Absorption with self is the prison of potential. As soon as you find out that helping someone else feels better than helping yourself you can begin to cure the "Why Me" Cancer. The people respected are those who have their

"me" in their back pocket. Get it?? They are always sitting on their "Me"....

When you finally "get it" you will see how great you can be by just being a "me" who doesn't think about "me" any longer. It is a calling to find your uniqueness and apply it to helping others for whom your uniqueness is special. Your crippled hand becomes powerful and unseen and appreciated. That is all one can ask of life.

Find your Truth.

Write your book.

Start wiping the tears of others.

You will then know "Why Me?"

Last Chapter

We all reach the same end.

Though we journey through life as if we were the central actor in our unique video. But we all end up in the same place... putting Faith aside....

We live as if we will never end. Even old people are still just the young people they always were. Look at them together and they are talking freely with lots of laughter... if... medical circumstances are okay....

Could we have done more and better?? Sure. Are there private things done that were not good? That may have hurt someone else? For most... yes. No one escapes the brush with sin and Evil and self-centeredness.

Something tells you that your vigorous days are numbered. Everything changes to grey. You see more clearly. Wisdom unseen until now.

If you are out of self, you will see so much that needs to be done. Encouraging moral certitude. Warning and guiding

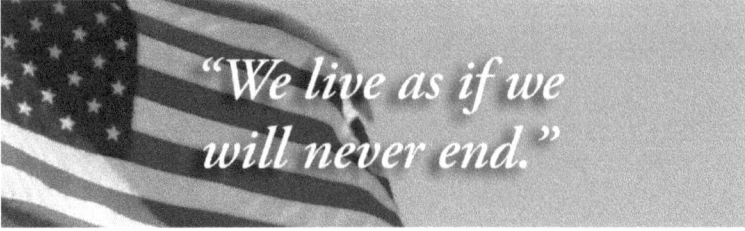

"We live as if we will never end."

everyone you still can, especially strangers…. Strangers can only judge your caring….

If you believe in God. Then say it! May you not encounter one person not hearing your parting words…"God Bless You."

Do good till your last breath.

Serve others as their waiter of Truth.

Die in love with God.

What's the point otherwise?

BREAKING
NEWS

"And the seas parted"

And spared us the unbiased reporting on stiletto heels and empathy from our elite bigoted experts.

Thousands of rafts and flat bottom fishing boats crisscrossing every neighborhood in Houston, hundreds of square miles in search of the stranded.

"Hello?? Anyone there??" Black, white, Democrat, Republican, firemen, National Guard, and anonymous citizens became the unified army against tragedy. Amazing beautiful stuff.

I am sure we will find people to blame as that is our disgusting game. Who did what when and soon or big enough? The average guy could care less about all that... He knows it's a waste of time.

Bass Pro Shops offered assistance and flatboats! To see the quiet individual and corporate America shake hands is what our great nation is all about. Stop criticizing her, for God's sake...

Hey, maybe we should flood the halls of congress so they can take off their stupid hats and swim back and forth helping one another reach dry land exhausted and united. So we can be proud of them.

The flood gates of hope have been opened.

"Oh....say can you see?"....

EPILOGUE

It has taken over 4 years to write these 12 books. Over 800 chapters. Nothing has been planned. It just happens with impulse at this keyboard. It is honest and spontaneous. Go figure?

With all that is recently happening in politics and the media these unrelated short blogs have become more relevant than I imagined. Started on a whim as short blogs they have become powerful silent screams of perilous times ahead. Very perilous. Danger is everywhere. I am scared.

We are allowing everything fundamental to our successes to be slandered and disavowed. Our children and future generations will be denied the taste of freedom and fairness we have fought for.

The "New Fairness" is all about sensitivity. This is a false god. Entitlement is a false god. Chaos is at our doorsteps.

Only you and I can stop it by voting on everything we can.

Hate is being fueled by ignorance and emotion.

Is this our call to arms??

PhotoLog

Why Die – Chapter 11

ASPCF – Chapter 22

Luvtrievers – Chapter 24

Bomb – Chapter 29

Eyes On - Chapter 31

Flag And Cross – Chapter 36

Patriotic Duty – Chapter 54

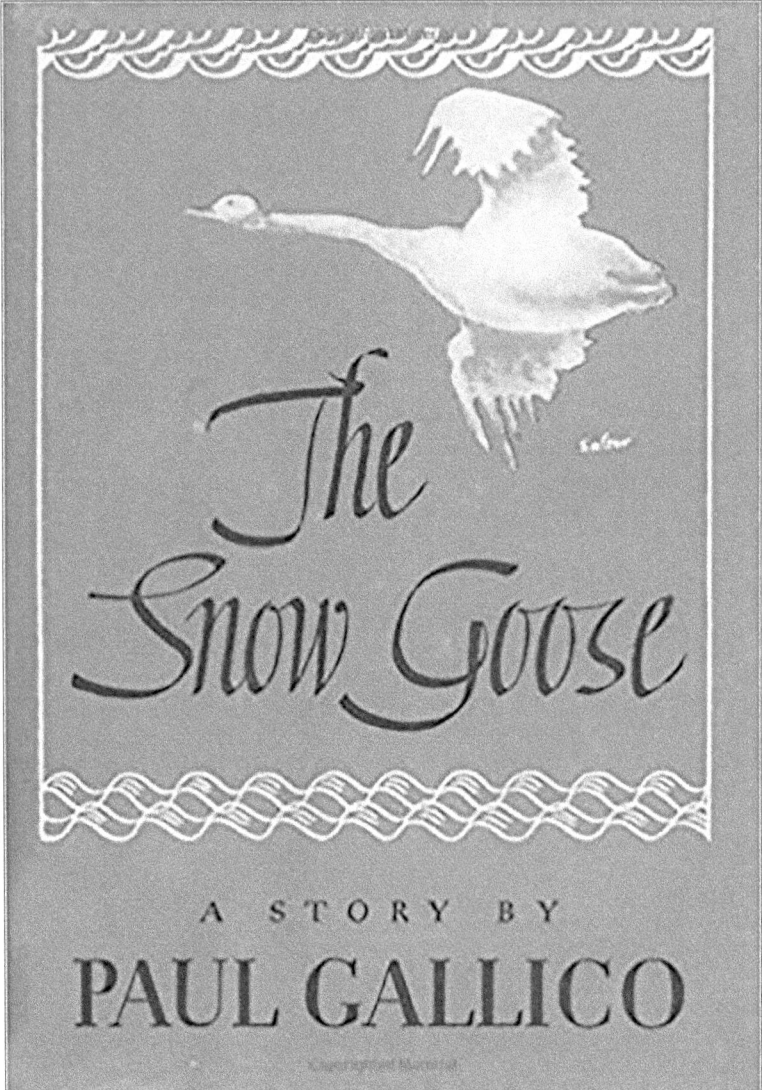

THE
SNOW GOOSE

A STORY BY
PAUL GALLICO

Broken Wings – Chapter 67

A Buddy Died – Chapter 76

The Blacksmith - Chapter 88

ACKNOWLEDGEMENTS

In a way I have to acknowledge all of you. I am concerned for your safety and future. If we don't return to proven values then war is inevitable.

Families matter. Our grandchildren and great-great-great grandchildren deserve that we solve our problems now.... and not pass them on. We are looking down the barrel of evil and self-centeredness.

I would not be putting myself out there for you and my family if I did not care. Please read every chapter privately, please. Then you will be armed.

My short list of contributors:

There are my daughters, Candice and Courtney, who thought they knew their dad, but really didn't. There is my brilliant wife Christina, who thought she knew her husband.... And then there are my friends from the past whose life journeys I do not fully know, and who do not know me now. For in life it is who we become, not who we were.

Then there are the men of my "No Walls" Bible Studies and Max Lucado who freed us to think with assurance and humility, leading me to new friendships of the highest quality.

There are the veterans I served with and those I didn't. Ames, Riojas, Stevens, Cleary, Fry, Ross, Hawes, Hawkins, Bisset, Hernandez, Bruton, Olson, Vecchione, Phillips, Waddell and my brothers in BUD/S 31E, and countless others ... where bonding and trust was defined.

Lastly, there are Sandra Simmons-Dawson and Brian Dawson who helped edit and format the books, website, and marketing. Their firm, Money Management Solutions, Inc. dba Customer Finder Marketing https:// CustomerFinderMarketing.com/ is a gem.

IN THE WORDS OF OTHERS

Reviews for 1-800-I-Am-Unhappy
(Volumes 1 and 2)

"This is a book by a man of many directions and passions. Straightforward yet thought provoking. Loyal to his convictions and country. And brave. Sharing. Warrior. Humanitarian."

Jeff Lytle, Editorial Page Editor, Naples Daily News

"As a friend, Chris has helped me understand the inherent conflicts embedded in the language of 'political correctness' and how it attempts, and frequently succeeds, in disguising and defeating the 'truth.' Chris is engaged in a rhetorical battle — we need his insight."

William Lord, a 32-year-veteran Executive Producer and Vice-President of ABC News, and Professor of Journalism at Boston University

"Chris writes like he lives. As a man of distinction, he is a voice for the poor, a champion of the truth and a friend of strong character and conviction. His word and his service are a blessing to all who encounter him."

Vann R. Ellison, President/CEO, St. Matthew's House, Inc.

"My nickname for Chris is "Dream-Catcher"- because that's who he is to me. He is my mentor in how to give on His behalf. Freely and generously, Chris offers both words, "God bless you!", and gifts. And all the while he is making a compelling and powerful statement. Chris Bent has discovered a beautiful way to live!"

Rev. Dr. Ruth Merriam,
The Church on the Cape (U.M.C.), Cape Porpoise, Maine

"Chris Bent is a very unusual person – Navy SEAL, Yale graduate, successful business owner, and radical Christian who is comfortable talking with anyone at any level in society. He doesn't just talk about faith or caring about the poor, Chris actually lives his faith and he works with the poor. His smile is genuine and reflects his deep joy in life, America, hard work, people and (most definitely) God. I have enjoyed reading his writings; they are different, often hard hitting and sometimes maybe even a little wild. Each one gives a fresh perspective on contemporary lives, reflecting Chris' intel- ligence and faith. Chris enjoys moving mountains."

Rev. Dr. Ted Sauter, Senior Pastor, North Naples United Methodist Church

Reviews for 1-800-For-Women-Only

"It is amazing that a man would want to write about women. That is a change, but Chris has a sense of humor that can make you laugh. Women will enjoy this book and men may gain new insight."

Dorothy K. Ederer, O.P., Director of Campus Ministry,
St. John Student Center, East Lansing, Michigan

"Light, refreshing take on some not so light topics. Wrapped in silliness and wit are serious, social and moral truths that challenge us to be more than ordinary."

Peggy Ryba, Membership Director, North Naples Church, Naples, Florida

"Chris is like a modern day prophet, throwing modern day concepts and concerns out there for us to contemplate. The seeds he tosses can land on sand or soil depending on the reader. I suggest you pull up a nice spot in your garden and sit down and read…then allow some of his thoughts to germinate in your life! "

Mia Guinan, Owner, Gourmet Gang, Camp Trident, Virginia Beach VA

"1-800-For-Women-Only or the "Mystery of Women" is interesting because it is brutally accurate. In fact, it is frightening to read the explanations of characteristics of women. Many of these things I had not even been aware of, but they are "right on target". The book is written with great sensitivity and insight. I never got the feeling that women were criticized, but accepted as observed. It is an easy fun read and a great gift to give to a friend or even a son who is even thinking of getting married. As the mother of three sons, I know it is true; "Heart-felt is at the core of being. Being somebody."

Sue Lester, Volunteer, Children's Coalition of
Collier County, Pilot Club, Naples, Florida

"Chris Bent's extraordinary life has given him a perspective that so very few have. His insight comes not only from his incredible experiences but from his deeply rooted sense of responsibility, caring, and love for others. His thoughtful mind is not on idle, but instead always on overdrive, crystallizing in well thought out words those concepts that would have many times escaped us, were it not for the efforts of this author to engage, care deeply, and then, as Chris has done so remarkably here, write."

Jennifer L. Whitelaw, Attorney, Whitelaw Legal Group, Naples, FL

Reviews for 1-800-Laughing-Out-Loud

"Chis is a stew: meat, potatoes, veggies, gravy, biscuits and mustard. A warm, tender mix of good taste, generous servings, and something for all appetites! Chris mixes a Hunter S. Thompson "Gonzo Journalism" writing style with a Soupy Sales "Pie in the Face" sense of humor. Chris writes about: Life Values, Family, Self, Respect, Good & Evil. His perspective of life's Value Proposition engages our brain to think about ourselves and others. Chris' previous books are from the Heart and Soul. Take his counsel of his life's experience. There is good advice in each chapter! You will enjoy each word like every bite of a good stew."

Gerry Ross, Executive, Pratt & Whitney (Retired)

"Chris Bent is the type of guy you want to share a cold beer with at the end of a lousy day and have him philosophize on the real meaning of life. Since you might not have that opportunity anytime soon let me suggest you read 1-800-LAUGHING-OUT-LOUD. Perfect title for the book, because when reading it you will."

Nancy Lascheid, RN, BSN, Co-Founder,
Neighborhood Health Clinic, Naples, Florida

Reviews for 1-800-Oh-My-Goodness

"With 1-800-Oh-My-Goodness, Chris Bent offers his thoughts on a variety of topics, in order to amuse, inspire, and challenge any reader. With his witty insight, and perspective forged from life experience, Chris seeks to help us all become better individuals."

Michael Hopkins, Attorney, Naples, FL

"In this book Chis is honest and open with the reader. He definitely gives you a lot to ponder. You can't wait to see what he is going to share next."

Dorothy K. Ederer O.P., Director of Campus Ministry,
St. John Student Center

"Oh my goodness", Chris has again presented a faith filled and thought provoking book. His stream of thought, that often reads more like poetry than prose, will cause you to rethink moments of life in a context of love and promise."

Rev Jean Moorman Brindel, CFRE, AFP,
Associate Director of Development,
Emeritus United Theological Seminary, Dayton Ohio

"Honest, incisive, poetic and profound: the writings of Chris Bent. Passion for people, the nation and the world spring from his pages; provocative questions leap from the shortest chapters ever. Silent voices speak in these pages and nothing is to be taken for granted, for life and love run deep between the lines of 1-800-Oh-My-Goodness. "

Wendy J. Deichmann, PhD, President, United Theological Seminary

Reviews for 1-800-For-SEALS-Only

"Pungent, cogent, wistful, idealistic, naive, wise, — all in no particular sequence, reflecting a view of life that it is all unpredictable, and it is mental, physical & moral preparation that will sustain us… there are life lessons and observations here for anyone and everyone…."

Lt (jg) James Hawes, BUDS 29E, SEAL, CIA, (He was the First SEAL In Africa)…(sadly was my UDTR Instructor too)

"Who knew SEALs could write? (LOL) But what Chris does with his gift is really less "writing" than it is expressing the "unwritten." We all have our thoughts; and Frogmen have certain very special and unique shared experiences. Chris puts the pen to the task of relating what we (the Frogs) have experienced and what we (all of his readers) now observe in sharing the experience of the world around us. It's challenging and funny (if you've been through a "real Hell Week"), and sometimes sad. But hey, isn't life? Hooyah!"

Timothy Phillips, SEAL, BUDS 166, ST-8, ST-4

"Chris - great stuff…as always. "Hooyah Mike"…"Every sin is a grenade"…"My wife is my swim buddy"…great thoughts as only a SEAL can put into words. I love it and will BUY a few copies for my Assistant Sergeant at Arms to read to guide their young lives… Hooyah Chris and see you soon!"

Phil King, Sergeant at Arms, NC Senate, BUDS 32

"Mr. Bent's words of wisdom on some of the evolutions of U. S. Navy SEAL training are demonstrated to apply to everyday life with such simplicity. God, Family, Country, is the essence of being an honorable and patriotic American. It is the ethos of the Navy SEAL credo. The band of brothers whose lives are bonded as one in being; all for one and one for all! Nothing in this world feels better to receive in life as the emblem, the SEAL Trident, of a true warrior and to receive into one's heart the holy trinity! Hooyah! The only easy day was yesterday!"

Erasmo Elijah Riojas (Doc Rio) HMC (SEAL) Ret.

"I am a SEAL Teammate of LT. Chris Bent. During our years of serving our country as Naval Special Warfare Operatives, Chris always manifested that "Can Do" attitude so necessary for success in what many would consider: "A tough way to make a living!"

Among other sub-specialties, Chris and I had the honor of being the Platoon Commanders who would "Recover Astronauts!" Within the pages of "1-800-FOR-SEALS-ONLY", you will get to see the mind-set of students going through BUDS Training (still the toughest Military Training in the World) with most Classes experiencing an over 80% Drop Out Rate! Chris masterfully combines our training to current issues existing today. A Giant HOOYAH for a must read publication! 1-800-FOR-SEALS-ONLY is awarded a big BRAVO ZULU from your old Teammates!"

Dr. Frank Cleary, OIC, Seventh Platoon, ST-2 (Ret.)

"Five Stars for the FROGFATHER! This is a great book, and should be required reading...."

Commander (SEAL) Tom Hawkins, USN, Ret., author, NSW Historian

"Chris Bent has again taken his many and varied life experiences and applied them to life in general and "how to do it right". This book is clearly for everyone, not just SEAL's. Life was never meant to be easy and all of us can take away something from this book and the Frogman saying "The only easy day was yesterday". Even if it is the hard way....do the right thing.

From one Frogman to another I say to Chris, your eulogy (chapter 75) should be read when the time comes: Teammate, seen or unseen, you truly have made a difference!

Hooyah 1-800-For-SEALS-Only!"

Mike Macready, SEAL Team One, BUD/S 49 West Coast

"Chris Bent's latest 1-800 offering certainly gets my SEAL of approval... Using his own unique blend of insight, intellect and inspiration, Chris lifts parallels from the rich history and tradition behind the US Navy SEALs to provide challenging questions and equally thought provoking answers to this experience that we call life. In this social-networking, politically-corrected day and age where common sense, discipline and values seem to have fallen by the wayside, Chris Bent cuts through like a K-Bar to remind us all exactly what is of the utmost importance."

Darren A. Greenwell - NSW Historian, Researcher, Collector

Reviews for 1-800-For-Veterans-Only

"I will always have a special place in my heart for our veterans. Growing up in a military family, I spent my childhood years living on various Air Force bases, learning the lingo, and exploring the far corners of the world while my father flew various missions in both peacetime and conflict. This upbringing has given me a love and appreciation of anything written about the military, whether it be a Tom Clancy thriller or a World War II biography. Author Chris Bent has written some wonderful books in the past few years and I simply love his latest, "1-800-For-Veterans-Only".

Bent definitely has a way with words and his short essays on a variety of topics are conversational, often very witty, and sometimes quite touching. There are so many things that are touched on in this read that it would be impossible not to strike a chord with someone who has had any connection to the military over their lifetime, myself included. From thoughts on enlisting, experiences at boot camp, early days in the service and the uncertainties faced, to the battleground itself. Bent discusses not only what it's like to come home after a deployment, but the experiences of being a veteran and some of the darker aspects of this that we see in our country today.

One of the things that I found most inspiring about Bent's latest was his ability to speak directly to those veterans who may be out there and possibly struggling. There is some very sage wisdom in this one and it certainly has the potential to turn some lives around. Very well done."

TFL READER – Amazon Book Reviewer

A Veteran's Comment on the Chapter "The Hand"

"I agree because when this USMC veteran returned home there were no handshakes or high fives but plenty of shaken fists.

I'm reminded of a verse from "Where No One Stands Alone"

"Hold my hand all the way every hour every day

From here to the great unknown

Take my hand let me stand

Where no one stands alone."

There are two photos of hands representing two distinct eras: The first is a stained glass window in a Chapel at Paris Island. S.C., with The Hand of God holding 12 Marines from my unit who were killed on Jan. 20, 1968 in Quang Tri Province, Vietnam.

The second is a marble work entitled "Hand in Hand" that stands at the entrance of a children's rehabilitation clinic in Dong Ha, Vietnam, just a few miles from the site where the above Marines were killed."

Floyd Killough, USMC (Ret.)

Reviews for 1-800-Oh-My-Blackness

"Chris, just got finished reading your chapters. A lot to digest, but so much of it, if not all of it, point on. I'm flattered that Nancy thinks this highly of me to offer you my opinion. What stuck out the most in the reading was values and respectability. I try to teach the young people I mentor the three "Rs", reliability, respectability, and responsibility.

Adam bomb was the bomb, I hope I'm hunched over with pride helping others."

Harold G Weeks, President, Naples NAACP

"I am a black man... better stated "am a man in black skin".

Chris, you capture and present a view of the uncolored spirit that lives inside. You have captured the unique way to challenge the heart with the eyes, the eyes with the morals, the soul with the flesh and essence of survival with eventual death if we continue to turn a blind eye to the truth that screams for change. The eyes that read this book will be forever changed. The mind will question. Long established misconceptions will be reevaluated. And hopefully change how we view, treat and learn from those born with differences."

Vernon K. Jackson

Reviews for 1-800-Only-For-Love

"I started reading 1-800-Only-For-Love. I have put it down only to let you know how powerful I think it is. Just half way through it and it brings tears to my eyes, chapter after chapter. I cannot tell you how much it mirrors my life.

We have often spoken about personal feelings and events in our lives and how similar they are. This book tells it all. What we have given up over the years in order to advance ourselves. Turning our backs on Love when really it has been what we lost, what we needed, and what we were searching for, even today.

I want to give my daughters, daughters-in-law, Ex-wife, and current roommate/girlfriend a copy to read. It says a lot that I cannot express for myself. Thanks and God Bless.

Lee Lyons – Naples, FL

Reviews for 1-800-Old People-Matter

"Despite the title, this book provides wisdom for all ages with the key message that a person's true beauty, strength, and age lies within. Worth a read."

Michael Hopkins, Attorney at Law, Naples, FL

Chris Bent has a real gift for writing thought provoking books with short chapters....each of which has humor, a catchy literary style, and a powerful message on which to reflect. Chris's overriding message is to live the Golden Rule, reaching out to assist others while also looking inward to address our own shortcomings. Collectively, his thoughts convey a clarion call for all of us to look beyond self-satisfaction and to focus on what we can do to help others and to better the world in which we live. Presented without espousing specific religious doctrine, his latest book is a page turner--always encouraging the reader to see what is next in Chris's captivating messages.

John E. Sampson, Retired Fortune 500 Senior Executive

There's a lot of wisdom within these pages. And, sad to say, who better to judge than us "old people."

Dr. Francis B. Cleary (Retired) Senior Dental Staff
and OPD Director, Hartford Hospital, Hartford, CT

www.ingramcontent.com/pod-product-compliance
Lightning Source LLC
Chambersburg PA
CBHW071523040426
42452CB00008B/862